New Jersey Law Enforcement Exam (LEE) Review Guide 2016

By Lewis Morris

ISBN-13: 978 1535231978
ISBN-10: 1535231971

DEDICATION

This Exam Review guide is dedicated to J.T. For your dedication to serving the good people of the City of New York

CONTENTS

ACKNOWLEDGMENTS

I would like to acknowledge the hard work and talent of Gabriella Morris who assisted with the editing and cover art for this edition.

About The Exam

The New Jersey Law Enforcement Exam (LEE) is the exam that helps select candidates for the following positions: The 2016 LEE announcement consists of the following titles: Municipal Police Officer, Campus Police Officer Recruit, County Police Officer, Park Police Officer, Police Officer Recruit Human Services, Police Officer Palisades Interstate Park, Sheriff's Officer, County Correction Officer, and Correction Officer Recruit Juvenile Justice.

For the latest information concerning the exam and registration visit the New Jersey Civil Service Commission at: http://www.state.nj.us/csc/about/news/safety/index.html

The New Jersey LEE is a 3-part examination with a 3 hour and 20-minute time limit to complete 169 items.

Each of the three parts are scored separately, then they are combined and weighted to produce a final average. A candidate who fails to meet the minimum passing score for any one of the three sections fails the entire exam. The exam is scaled and approximately 85% of the candidates who sit for the exam will pass.

Part 1 – Written Abilities/ Cognitive Section
The first part of the examination involves 48 multiple-choice questions (A thru D responses) designed to test the following sub areas: reading comprehension; written & oral expression; inductive reasoning; deductive reasoning; information ordering; and problem sensitivity. There are 8 questions for each of the 6 sub areas spread throughout this part of the exam. The questions on this section are typical of law enforcement exams. Each question has only one correct answer. There is no penalty for guessing wrong, and the candidate should leave no questions blank. It is recommended that a candidate spend 2 ½ hours of the exam on this section.

Part 2 – Work Styles Questionnaire

This section of the exam tests if an individual possesses certain attitudes and personality traits found to be suitable in a police officer. These questions are similar to career interest exams given by many career planning centers at colleges and trade schools. The *Work Styles Questionnaire* on the exam consists of 74 statements in which candidates are directed to read and determine how they "feel" the statement describes them. The answers are provided on a 1 thru 5 scale such as: (1) Strongly Disagree, (2) Disagree, (3) Unsure, (4) Agree, and (5) Strongly Agree. This section differs significantly from Part 1 since there are no right or wrong answers. The questions and responses for this section move quickly. The best way to mentally prepare for this type of exam is to begin thinking of yourself as a police officer. Try to view yourself as reliable, steady, courteous, assertive, and morally strong. When answering the questions, try to remain in that frame of mind.

Part 3 – Life Experience Survey

This section of the exam consists of 47 questions (A thru E choices) which the candidates are directed to select the answer choice that most accurately reports on the candidates' life experiences. This section is based on evidence that a person's past behavior is a reliable indicator of his or her future behavior. As with the *Work Styles Questionnaire*, there is no single right answer. There is a built in scale to detect deception and penalize a candidate who tries to pick the "best" response versus the most truthful response.

The exam is not considered difficult to pass, approximately 85% of the candidates completing the examination will receive a passing score. However, in order to get hired in such a competitive environment for such a desirable job, the candidate must score very close to 100%.

It is strongly recommended that you take as many law enforcement exams as possible prior to taking this exam. Practice and experience are your best ally in becoming a New Jersey law enforcement officer.

Requirements
Is there a minimum and maximum hiring age?
Yes, for all titles associated with the LEE, there is a minimum hiring age. Candidates need to be at least 18 years of age on or before the Closing Date shown on the examination announcement. The only title in the LEE announcement that has a maximum age is Municipal Police Officer. Applicants over age 35 as of the closing date of the examination are not eligible for Municipal Police Officer positions, with certain exceptions. (An applicant is considered to be over 35 the day after his/her 35th birthday.) By law, applicants may reduce their age by deducting the following: (1) the amount of their military service time that falls within the location and time limit criteria for New Jersey veteran's preference and/or (2) the amount of time previously served in certain law enforcement titles. To qualify for this provision, separation from prior service must have been for reasons other than removal for cause on charges of misconduct or delinquency. Please click here for the Municipal Police Maximum Hiring Age Information Sheet.

How can I get veteran's preference?
In order to be awarded veteran's preference, the appropriate documentation must be submitted and approved by the Department of Military and Veterans Affairs no later than 8 days prior to the issuance of an eligibility list.

Children of a deceased law enforcement officer, who was killed in the line of duty, receive preference in appointment second to that accorded to veterans pursuant to current law, but superseding that accorded to non-veterans. All duly qualified applicants whose natural or adoptive parent was killed in the lawful discharge of official duties while serving as a law enforcement officer in any law enforcement agency in the State at any time prior to the closing date for the filing of an application, provided that required documentation is submitted with the application by the closing date, shall be accorded this preference. This paragraph shall not, however, be applicable if the municipality has entered into a consent decree with the United States Department of Justice concerning the hiring practices of the municipality.

When a veteran and a non-veteran whose parent was killed in the lawful discharge of official duties while serving as a law enforcement officer in any law enforcement agency in the State are duly qualified applicants for a position, first preference shall be given to the veteran.

Do veterans get extra points?

No extra points are given to veterans. However, eligible candidates with disabled veteran or veteran status are grouped at the top of the certification list by their veteran status and then by their final averages. Disabled veterans are placed above veterans who, in turn, are placed ahead of non-veterans.

What is a certification?

It is a list of names selected from the eligible pool that the CSC provides to an Appointing Authority (AA) for a specific jurisdiction or agency to use for their hiring process. The certification lists candidates who pass the exam and ranks them based on their score in the following order: disabled veterans (ranked by score), veterans (ranked by score), and non-veterans (ranked by score). There is no hiring list or rank until a certification is requested by the AA for a hiring agency and the certification list is issued by the CSC.

Test Preparation Strategies

Beginning your Preparation

Begin preparing and studying as soon as possible. You want to engage your long term memory, which can only be done over a period of months.

Find a regular time in your schedule when you can devote a half an hour or more of quiet study time.

Set a schedule and stick to it. Discuss your schedule with your family so that everybody understands your need for uninterrupted study time.

Start practicing your memory skills in everyday life. If you are walking and see a billboard, take 10 seconds to look at it carefully. Then, as you go about your way, try to remember details such as color, names, and dates. If you take public transportation, there are numerous opportunities to practice this method because you have so many different advertisements to view.

Study without distractions to the best of your ability. Turn off your phone. Inform people close to you that you will be unavailable during that time so that there is no expectation of a returned phone call.

Be sure you are getting enough sleep. This can greatly affect your concentration and memory skills. Creating a peaceful sleep environment by eliminating lights and sounds, obtaining quality pillows, and limiting nighttime activities can help. You should not eat within an hour or so before bed, and avoid caffeine and chocolate several hours before bed.

Limiting or stopping alcohol use entirely will assist you concerning the New Jersey Law Enforcement vetting process. Alcohol can seriously affect your memory and concentration abilities in several specific ways. Being intoxicated has been proven to negatively affect abstract thinking skills in people for at least 6 weeks. Alcohol affects sleep by contributing to sleep apnea, and many people who drink only moderately have been shown to sleep poorly. Regular use of alcohol contributes to weight gain and raises blood pressure.

Motivate yourself. Find a way to be enthusiastic in your preparation. Prove to yourself that you can earn a high score and make the grade. Keep a positive outlook and make it a positive experience.

Start early. Begin preparing as soon as the exam is announced.

Avoid last minute cramming. Cramming does not work, but refreshing your memory on the night before the exam does.

Give yourself enough time to complete each sub area question set in a single seating. This will give you more confidence and provide you with a realistic expectation for the actual exam.

Develop careful reading habits. You must become an active reader. For example, rephrase each question in your own words to make sure you understand the question. Re-check your answers and make sure your choice correctly answers the question asked.

Don't try to memorize practice questions, instead focus on the process of reading critically and analyze each one.

Concentrate on the sections of the exam you find most challenging. Budget your time accordingly to practice more difficult areas.

* Focus on completing one sub area question set at a time. Go through your wrong answers and locate the correct answer by reading through the review material. Complete an error analysis early in your studying so that you can work through any deficiencies early enough to gain confidence in the material.

* Create a set of flash cards by taking any unfamiliar words from the glossary and putting them on index cards. Write out the definition on the reverse side of the card.

The Night Before the Exam

Briefly study and review the practice questions you have already completed.
Focus on your successful responses. Your goal is to refresh your memory and reduce anxiety. Set two alarm clocks and leave an hour or so before going to bed. Refrain from looking at a computer screen for at least an hour before bed because the type of light emitted from the screen can also contribute to sleeplessness.

Getting Ready the Day of the Examination

1. Stick to your normal routine as much as possible. Some suggestions may not be in your normal routine, but they usually allow most people to perform their best.

2. Get adequate sleep. Most adults do best with 7-8 hours. Adopt this pattern at least a week prior to the exam. Even if you have trouble sleeping the night before the exam, don't worry. As long as you have rested well for several days leading up to the exam, your body will adjust and your performance will remain high.

3. Get up early enough to have plenty of time to have a light, balanced breakfast. Set your alarm and have a backup alarm set as well.

4. Minimize the use of outside influences (food, caffeine, nicotine, entertainment, etc.) that might over or under stimulate you.

5. Leave for the test early enough to allow for the traffic, weather, and parking. Work out childcare needs well in advance. Give yourself ample time to settle in at the test site.
On the morning of the exam, log into a local traffic site, and consider using a traffic app such as "Waze" to keep updated on

traffic issues. Have somebody drive you to the test, or take public transportation if possible. Imagine how stressful it would be if you ran into traffic and then had to struggle to find parking.

* Eat before the test. Having food in your stomach will give you energy and help you focus, however avoid heavy foods which can make you groggy.

At the Exam Site

1. Listen to instructions and directions from hall monitors and test proctors. Make sure that you understand the instructions and ask questions at the designated time before the test begins if you are unsure of any aspect of what you should do during the test.

2. Use your time carefully. Do not rush. You should have enough time to cover the entire test if you move through it steadily, and do not spend too much time on any one question. Part I consists of questions you would expect to find on a law enforcement exam. Part II and Part III consist of questions that are short and quick. Work through these steadily, read them slowly enough to make sure you understand them, but without getting hung up any one question.

3. Read the questions and all the alternative answers carefully. Do not jump to an answer before you have completely read all of the alternatives.

4. Respond to each question separately. The answer to one question is not meant to lead you to another.

5. Answer all of the questions. Use your informed judgment to make a choice between alternatives. This may feel like an "educated guess" but to the extent that it is informed, you are demonstrating a degree of knowledge and not just blindly guessing.

6. Don't worry about trick questions. None of the questions in this test are designed to be a trick question. The test is really intended to allow you to demonstrate your understanding and skills on each sub-area. Avoid reading too much into a question.

* Go to the bathroom before walking into the exam room. You don't want to waste any time worrying about your bodily needs during the test.

Avoiding common mistakes on a bubble-type of answer sheet.

1. This type of answer sheet is called an "optical scan sheet". It is fed into a machine which quickly scores it. Any stray marks outside of the bubbles can create errors.
2. Make sure you use a #2 pencil. This is the most common type of pencil. Be wary of mechanical pencils, as the lead is sometimes harder and will not make a dark enough bubble which can even tear the paper.
3. Bubble in your answers very lightly at first. This way, if you make a mistake, you can erase it without leaving a mark. After you have completed the exam, then carefully darken in all of the bubbles to produce a uniform scan.
4. Make sure to fill in the bubble completely. Do not use checkmarks, dots, or an "X". The scanning machine will not pick it up.
5. Bring in several new pencils with fresh, clean erasers. Check the erasers on the pencils before the exam. If a pencil is old or poorly made, the eraser will be hard and create smudges when used. Check this beforehand.
6. Be very careful if you skip a question. If you do want to leave a question for later, make absolutely sure you keep the order correct. Double check this before moving on.
7. After every five questions stop and check your order. This way, if you have answered out of order, it will be easier to fix.
8. Fully darken in the circle, without damaging the paper.
9. Left handed people sometimes have a problem with their hand creating smudges. If this is the case, keep an eye on the bottom of your hand to make sure it is not picking up pencil graphite. If so, rub your hand to keep it clean. Adjust the paper so that the answer sheet remains smudge free.

Immediately after the exam

As soon as you finish, find a quiet space to sit down and record your thoughts and impressions about the exam. Write down as many specific things as you can. This will help you, should you desire to take a similar exam for a different law enforcement title. This exam is very similar in format and content to other exams you may later take. Recording your thoughts will assist you in developing an even better study plan for future exams.

Preparing for the Examination

Tests are given to assure selection of the most qualified persons into New Jersey Law Enforcement while providing all candidates a chance to compete fairly. New Jersey will use several kinds of tests and screening methods to gauge your readiness to become certified. The written exam is one component of the overall selection process. Knowing the rationale for this test and having a realistic perception of the job can improve your chance to better demonstrate your potential.

This test is designed to assess:

how well you reason and apply basic problem solving skills

your basic writing skills

your basic reading comprehension

how well your work preferences and experiences match those of people who have been successful in a community policing organization.

In the days and weeks before the exam these suggestions are offered:

1. Access the Preparation Guide online with the validation code which is issued to you when you register for the exam. Make sure you understand each step in the process so you can give optimum performance. Get a feel for what the job is really like for a new recruit, and visualize what it will be like to be a police professional.

2. Make sure that you accurately complete any forms or requirements prior to the exam.

3. Take some time every day to improve your reading and writing skills. These skills are important for effective performance as a Police Recruit and will be assessed by the test. Of course, these skills are also important in many other lines of work, including promotions within New Jersey Law Enforcement.

4. Practice taking other tests. This can reduce testing anxiety and improve your test taking strategies. The City of New York routinely offers School Safety, Traffic Agent, and Corrections exams on a walk in basis. Sign up for and take at least one of these prior to your Police exam. This will give you valuable insight to the testing process. Many of the questions are similar to the New Jersey LEE.

6. The more confident you are in your abilities, the better you will do on the exam. The way to become confident is to practice as many questions before the exam as possible. There is a very strong relationship between the number of practice questions completed and an individual's ability to perform well.

7. Strive to stay focused on the exam. Practice regaining focus

when you feel your mind wandering. Successful test-takers are aware of when their mind wanders and have strategies for regaining focus. It is also normal for negative, self-defeating thoughts to enter your mind after a series of difficult questions. The trick is to recognize this for what it is, and use a strategy for eliminating the negativity. One way is to create a positive image of relaxing on the couch, watching a favorite movie after the exam. Think to yourself "I am almost there. Let's get back in the game and do this. Then I can go home and relax". Positive imagery is very powerful.

Attitude. This exam is an opportunity for you to show your skills and abilities, and a positive attitude can have an impact on increasing your test score. There are a few ways to fine-tune your attitude about taking this exam:

Look at this exam as a challenge but try not to get stressed by thinking about it too much.
Remember that passing this exam is just one step in the selection process for entrance to the police department.

Understand the test format and requirements

1. Read all of the directions carefully.

2. Understand how to correctly use the bubble sheet. Ask for clarification if you do not understand how to take the examination.

3. Know that you have three hours and twenty minutes to complete the examination. You are responsible for monitoring your use of the allotted time. Bring a watch and monitor it.

Understand the test question
1. Read each question carefully. Try to answer the question before you look at the choices.
If you know the answer, compare it to the available choices and pick the choice closest in meaning to your answer.

2. Recognize and make note of qualifiers. Qualifiers are words that change a statement. Words like always, most, equal, good, and bad. In a multiple choice question, qualifiers can make an option on a test question be a correct option or an incorrect option. For example, the following two statements are nearly identical: It often rains in Los Alamos. It is always raining in Los Alamos. The first statement is true, while the word "always" in the second statement makes it false. Be aware of qualifiers that appear in a test question or in the answer choice.
To tackle qualifiers, you need to know the qualifier groups:
· All, most, some, none (no)
· Always, usually, sometimes, never
· Great, much, little, no
· More than, equal to, or less than
· Good, bad
· Is, is not
Whenever one qualifier from a group is used in an answer choice, substitute each of the others from the group. Then you can tell which of the qualifiers fits best. If the best qualifier is the one in the answer choice, then the choice is correct, if the best qualifier is another one from the family, then the answer choice is false.

3. Negatives are words like no, not, none and never, or they can be made by prefixes like il-, as in illogical, un-, as in uninterested, or im- as in impatient. Notice negatives because they can reverse the meaning of a sentence. For example, in this answer option, the prefix in- in incomplete causes the statement to be false: "Because he based his research on incorrect data, his argument was imperfect."

Proceed through the questions strategically

1. Do not get stuck on words or sentences you do not understand: You may still get the main idea of the sentence or paragraph without understanding the individual word or the meaning of a sentence.

2. Use the process of elimination. If you do not know the answer to a question, first eliminate those choices that are clearly incorrect. Then, put a mark next to each remaining choice to indicate what you think about it (e.g., maybe, likely, or probable).
This will save you time, particularly if you decide to skip the question and come back to it later, by reducing the number of answers you have to reread and re-evaluate before making your final choice.

3. Guess. There is no penalty for selecting an incorrect answer in this examination, so answer every question. If the examination period is about to end and you will not be able to complete all of the questions, reserve three to five minutes toward the very end of the test to answer these questions, even if you must guess.
While your guesses may not be all correct, the alternative is to leave these questions blank and receive no credit.

4. In "All of the above" and "None of the above" choices, if you are certain one of the statements is true don't choose "None of the above" or one of the statements are false don't choose "All of the above".

In a question with an "All of the above" choice, if you see that at there are least two correct statements, then "All of the above" is probably the answer.

How to avoid making errors

Each one of us has strengths and weaknesses concerning tests. This section will give you tools to identify and address weaknesses in your test-taking ability. The process of comparing your answers with the answer key and identifying patterns will help you tackle recurring problems with your testing skills.

The sample questions contained in each question type in this guide are very similar to the kinds of questions that will appear on the actual examination. Focus on the questions you got wrong. Read through the test taking strategies below and apply the strategies to help you avoid making the same mistakes in the future.

There are many possible reasons for choosing an incorrect answer. Seven common reasons along with suggestions to minimize repeating such errors are presented below.

Why we make incorrect responses

1. Bubble sheet errors. It is very easy to place marks in the wrong place or double bubble a question. Be mindful that your answers match the correct question order.

You may also miss questions because you failed to provide an answer or were forced to quickly select any answer (that is, guess) before time was called. If either of these situations happened, consider why. Possible reasons include:

a. You may have missed a question because you skipped it and failed to return to it later.

b. You may have "lost track of the time" and been unaware that the examination period was about to end before you could mark any remaining unanswered questions. Check your watch frequently so that you can keep track of how much time you have left.

c. You may have been forced to make guesses for questions placed toward the end of the examination because you spent too much time working on difficult questions earlier. Skipping questions that are hard may give you more time with later questions that you have a better chance of answering correctly.

d. You may have skipped difficult questions but in returning to them did not save yourself time by reducing the number of answer choices (e.g., maybe, likely, or probable).

2. Misreading a question or answer by overlooking a key word or phrase. Because the exam is on a computer screen, you will not be able to underline key terms and phrases. Use your finger to underline a key term or phrase. It will not show up on the screen, but the physical act of tracing an imaginary line under the term or phrase will make it stand out in your mind.

3. Not knowing the meaning of one or more key terms.
When you encounter a word you don't know the meaning of, reread the sentence. Try to understand the general meaning of the sentence or paragraph. The meaning of the word should become clear once you understand the general meaning of the sentence around it. Study the glossary, as it will give you a solid working background of law enforcement terms.

4. Having difficulty telling the difference between the important and unimportant parts of a question because it is complicated or difficult to understand.
Try to break up the question into smaller parts; then concentrate on one part at a time. Read the possible answers before reading the questions. This helps you to direct your concentration while reading the question. Also, focus on the topic sentences that are usually the first and last sentences in a question. Read these difficult questions twice.

The first time, read for the general idea. Do not waste time on challenging words or phrases you do not understand. The second time, read for more detailed understanding. Finally, try to visualize what the question is asking by drawing a mental picture of what is going on in the question.

5. Not knowing how to combine different types of information. This is a problem of re-arranging information in the correct way so that it makes sense. Use your finger to underline important pieces of information in the question on the screen and then compare this information with the possible answers point-by-point. Concentrate on eliminating the wrong answers first.

6. Choosing an answer simply because it looks good. We call this type of mistake a "Red Herring". Several factors may cause you to choose a Red Herring are:

a. An incorrect answer may contain exact wording from the original question.

b. An incorrect answer may contain a phrase or sentence from the original question but presented in a different way. For example, a fact that is negated in the question may be presented as positive in an answer choice.

c. An incorrect answer may overstate the question's premise. For example, if the question states, "Some perpetrators...," the incorrect answer may state, "All perpetrators ...."

Some strategies for avoiding the tendency to select a "Red Herring" include:

a. Come up with your own answer before you review the answer choices. This will make you less likely to choose an answer that just "looks good."
b. Rate the likelihood of each probable answer before choosing one. Think in terms of "That's it!", "Probable", "Not Likely", "No Way!".

c. Beware of choosing answers based on common sense or previous knowledge and experience. Answer only on the basis of the material presented in the test question itself. In this sense, your experience can work against you.

d. Stick strictly to the facts or rules described in the test question itself. Carefully watch out for words such as "only," "never," "always," "whenever," "all," etc. and if you see one of these terms, take a few seconds to check that you understand the implications of the word in the question.

e. Beware of answers containing exact words or phrases from the question material. Do not assume that such answers are correct.

f. Prepare an inner dialogue to defend for your answer choice. Find something in the test question that will allow you to give a strong defense for your particular answer choice. How would you explain your answer to another person?

7. You may not know why you missed a question. If you just do not know why you missed a question, we suggest you review the preparation guide again. Also, talk with someone else who may be taking the test to compare answers and information or ask a tutor, friend, or a family member for help.

Summary:
* Read the question before you look at the answer.

* Come up with the answer in your head before looking at the possible answer. This way, the choices given on the test won't throw you off.

* Eliminate answers you know aren't right.

* Read all the choices before choosing your answer.

* There is no guessing penalty, so always take an educated guess and select an answer.

* Don't keep on changing your answer. Usually, your first choice is the right one, unless you misread the question and have become certain of the answer.

How to beat Testing Anxiety

What is Testing Anxiety?
Test anxiety is a nervousness that arises from the test situation. Our bodies produce chemical and physical changes in response to stress. In a sense, testing anxiety is our body's way of telling us that something really important is about to happen. As a result of this heightened state of readiness and awareness, we feel the pressure of the upcoming exam in many ways that can cause unease and discomfort. At times, these feelings may become overwhelming and negatively affect the test-taker's performance on the exam.

What causes testing anxiety?
The pressure to get a good grade, the high-stakes nature of an exam, the perceived difficulty of the exam, and the cost of the exam all contribute to the feelings of test anxiety.

What are the physical symptoms of testing anxiety?
- sweating palms and forehead
- sore neck and back from tense muscles
- headache
- nausea
- increased heart rate
- difficulty sleeping

What are the mental symptoms of testing anxiety?
- anger
- being frustrated with family, friends, and coworkers
- mental blocking (drawing a "blank" on questions)
- having difficulty focusing on exam questions during the test
- feeling sleepy and yawning during the exam
- doing poorly on an exam, even though you were confident in the material
- having difficulty remembering the definitions of key terms during the exam
- impaired concentration and inability to focus during the exam

- negative thoughts invade your thinking

How can I reduce testing anxiety?

- Practice, Practice, Practice. With enough practice answering similar questions, you will become desensitized to some of the anxiety producing stimuli.
- Learn the material over a long period of time vs. attempting to "cram" for the exam. By studying material over a month or more, you will engage your long-term memory. This type of memory is less affected by testing anxiety.
- Duplicate the testing environment as closely as possible and practice in that environment.
- Visit the testing site if possible.
- Take similar exams prior to taking your exam. (For example, take an upcoming corrections officer exam a month or two before the police exam. This will boost your confidence and desensitize you to anxiety producing stimulus. It will also familiarize you with testing policies and increase your stamina).
- learn to focus on the material by centering on important terms and concepts from the glossary and practice questions.
- create a detailed study plan and schedule
- organize your study materials to eliminate frustration looking for them
- learn and utilize relaxation techniques such as stretching, breathing, posture, and walking

How can controlling the study environment help manage testing anxiety?

- Set up your study environment so that it is conducive to learning and reduces stress. Find an area that has no interruptions or noise.
- Set up lighting so that there are no shadows or excessive brightness that cause squinting or straining of eye muscles. If possible, add an incandescent cool white bulb to the lighting to help balance the colors.
- Control the temperature so you are comfortable but alert.

- Choose a chair that is not too comfortable to cause drowsiness and has a straight back to enhance postural breathing.
- Do not study in bed. Your brain is conditioned to sleep in bed and your sessions will not be as productive. Your sleep may also be disturbed by studying prior to sleep.
- Have everything necessary to work close at hand.

How can I prepare for testing anxiety?
- Recognize it as a serious part of test preparation
- Develop a study plan and stick to it
- Study long-term over a period of a month or more
- Stay positive
- Take things day by day, one step at a time
- Learn an effective strategy for actively chasing away negative thoughts. Practice how to recognize them and have a specific, positive visual image to confront them with.
- Don't worry! Worrying is a waste of time and energy. As soon as you begin to feel worried, grab a book and do a few easy practice questions to move forward and boost confidence.

How do I confront testing anxiety when it occurs during the test?
- Stay engaged during the exam. Force your mind to focus.
- Slow down. Anxiety changes our perception of time and tends to cause rushing.
- Breathe. Practice sitting straight with good posture and breathe deeply and slowly. If necessary, purse your lips while exhaling to reduce your breathing rate.
- Feeling tense can be helpful. Recognize that it is your body gearing up to do its best.
- Stay in control.
- The exam will pass quickly enough. Your job is to slow things down and stay in the game as long as possible.

How can I use positive self-talk to manage testing anxiety in the future?
After the exam, write down your feelings. Focus on the positive

elements of the experience. This will most likely not be the last test you take in your life, and creating a positive image in your mind will help you minimize test anxiety in the future. Focus on positive self-statements such as "I Did It!", "It wasn't that bad", "Studying really helped.", "Some of the questions were challenging, but almost fun.", and "The test was like a puzzle to solve".

How can goal-setting help me manage or eliminate testing anxiety?
- Keep your goals realistic for studying. It is easy to be too optimistic about how much time you can devote to studying. When you can't study as much as you planned, it is then easy to become discouraged.
- Be sure your goals are your own. Don't allow friends and family to pressure you into something you don't really want to do.
- Try not to juggle too many goals at one time. If you want to prepare for an important exam, try putting off other major commitments until the exam has passed.
- Write your goals down. Be specific here. Describe in detail what you want to accomplish and what you are willing to do to earn this achievement. Try to keep a journal. In the journal, log your experiences and time studying. Record your thoughts and "A-ha! moments" as you learn along the way.
- Your goals should all have a definite expiration date.
- All goals should be as specific and measurable as possible. There should be an exact, concrete outcome in mind. For example, a goal might be: "I will earn a score of at least 98% on the 2015 administration of the New Jersey LEE". This goal has a specific, measurable outcome with a clear expiration date.

How can effective time-management help us eliminate testing anxiety?
- Begin by charting and calculating where your time goes every day. Chart what you do for a week. Look for dead spaces in time. Do you watch TV for a few hours a day? How much time do you spend on Facebook? Perhaps you like to watch a lot of sports and commentary. Also, find out

how much time you spend sleeping and getting ready. Investigate if there are people in your life who occupy your time. Once you have identified areas of your day that are not used efficiently, look for ways to limit the time lost and begin using it to study. After careful evaluation, you will be amazed at how much free time you actually have to use studying.

- Buy a day planner and chart out all of your responsibilities. Carry this with you everywhere. Complete it in pencil, and do not feel bad if you have to adjust it. Even if you find yourself wasting time here or there, record it. Look for areas of time you currently waste, and fill it with more productive time spent studying.
- Keep an eye out for procrastination. It is easy to get lazy or be afraid. The way to manage this is to start with an easy, short question set. Start with five or ten questions at a time. Slowly build up your study sessions until you are able to work for the entire test length without difficulty.
- Learn how to say "NO" to friends, family, and coworkers. "Time-Burglars" are everywhere. Look out for them and keep them at bay. Learn how to return calls when no one will answer so you can leave a voicemail that says "sorry I didn't call you sooner, I was studying……". Tell people what you are planning for and promise to be around after the test.
- Put your phone on silent for the time you are studying.
- Schedule ahead. Make a list of important events that are coming up and plan to study around them.
- Work backwards from the test date in your planning. First, black out any important dates such as holidays or family events. Then plan for short study and practice sessions. If possible, plan back a month or more.
- Also plan specific time to practice relaxation and fitness. Schedule regular stretching, yoga, or walking. Plan your meals carefully. This is not the time to start a drastic weight-loss program. It is the time to plan regular, nutritious meals that will support your learning and memory. Foods high in energy and healthy fats should be included. Foods high in processed sugar should be avoided.

- By planning your time wisely, you may find that studying actually buys you more "free" time and less wasted time.

How do we manage the effects of perfectionism or obsessing over the exam?

Some test-takers have the tendency to obsess over an exam. This obsession could be a strong motivator to study, but oftentimes, it becomes paralyzing. If this speaks to you, you are going to have to learn how to moderate your feelings. By scheduling thoughtful blocks for studying and then learning how to clear your mind, you will have a better chance of overcoming this. When setting a goal, define what result you are aiming for, and then decide what you are willing to put in to achieve the goal. Once set, stick to the plan and learn how to be satisfied with your effort.

How do we overcome procrastination?

Most people procrastinate. Very few people can self-start consistently day in and day out. For some people, however, procrastination is paralyzing and persistent. There are several reasons for procrastination:

- Time management. Many people just can't seem to balance their schedule to allot consistent time for studying. By the time they sit down to study they are exhausted or they are too wrapped up in their affairs to concentrate.
- Negative beliefs or emotions. Perhaps you performed poorly on another exam recently. The bad feelings and fear of failure drive you to delay working.
- Feeling overwhelmed. The exam seems too big and complex.
- Personal problems. Marriage, health, job situation, and finances.
- Difficulty concentrating. This issue can have many causes including diet, sleep, and outside stress. Learning how to control the physical environment is key to overcoming this issue.
- Boredom. Let's face it, studying is rarely thrilling. The way to overcome this is to start with short sessions and increase the study time as you go along.
- Fear of failure. Many people allow themselves to quit before they even start.

Why doesn't cramming work well?
Cramming is defined as studying intensely just prior to an exam. It generally includes an unfocused, disorganized, last-ditch attempt to learn material covered over a long period of time. Cramming often results in sleep deprivation, exhausted eyes, and an overwhelmed short-term memory. Often times, a test-taker will study the entire night before and arrive at the test site weary and unable to focus. Beyond the physical discomfort of cramming, there are very good reasons for spreading out studying from a brain function and memory point of view. Successful test-takers know that the long term memory is engaged during an exam. The only way to develop long-term memory of subject matter is to study over a long period of time.

What is the difference between short-term and long-term memory?
Short-term memory is also called "working memory". It is used when actually doing something or performing a skill. Testing engages long-term memory and is best developed over a period of weeks or months.

When we cram, what information is remembered, and what is forgotten?
Cramming has been well-studied. It is very clear that while cramming, the first and last items are remembered, while the material studied during the middle of the session is forgotten. The speed at which a person reads is also significant. The slower the reading, the more material is remembered. Also, if the reader pauses regularly to mentally restate what was read, the retention of information will be better.

What is the serial position effect?
The serial position effect is the tendency of a person to best recall the first and last items in a series, but forget the middle items. This effect is most apparent during cramming. When charted, the amount of retained material forms a reverse bell-shaped curve with the beginning and end retained the most.

What is the primacy effect?
This is the tendency for the first items presented in a series to be remembered better or more easily than those presented later in the series. If you hear a long list of words, it is more likely that you will remember the words you heard first (at the beginning of the list) than words that occurred in the middle.

Why does reading slowly while help?
Reading slowly while studying can help you retain more information because there is a tendency to repeat and rehearse the material. This will help you process the material to a deeper level and retain more.

If you must cram, what are some tips?
- Study the most important information first and last. Study the least important information in the middle.
- Draw up a clear plan and break your studying up into segments.
- Focus on key terms and vocabulary
- Read slowly. This will help you retain more information.

What about rumors?
Looking online at forums about the exam can be informative and helpful. Be careful, however, not to buy into the negativity that also exists on the forums. I recommend not visiting them for a few weeks leading up to the exam. It is too easy to get "psyched out" and start second-guessing yourself.

Can I "Beat" a test?
Simply put, *No.* The exam is professionally made and extensively field tested. The only way to beat the test is to practice numerous similar questions and, if possible, take similar exams such as the Traffic Agent, Court Officer, or School Safety Agent exams. Practice and experience are key.

How do I overcome negative thoughts?
When under stress, it is completely natural to experience negative thoughts. The key to overcoming these thoughts is to first recognize them when they occur, and second, have a specific visualization to focus on when the negative thoughts occur. For example, if you hit a hard string of questions, you might begin thinking that you are going to fail. Try to imagine yourself back at home in a few hours, eating your favorite take-out food, watching your favorite movie.
Visualization is an effective method for reducing anxiety, especially when combined with physical relaxation techniques such as deep breathing, stretching, or yoga. The more specific and focused your imagery is, the more effective it will be.

What about yoga, deep breathing, posture, and walking?
Relaxation strategies can be very effective at relieving testing anxiety. Learning how to breathe properly and keep good posture during the exam will increase your energy levels. If you are studying and begin to feel stressed, learn several slow stretches that help your posture and keep your back muscles supple. Yoga can be very beneficial, but you don't have to go out and join a studio. Start simple and incorporate balance into your routine.

Testing Anxiety Assessment Tool

Read through the responses below and assign a "0,1, or 2" indicating the degree this statement reflects your feelings, 0 being none and 2 being great. Keep in mind that questions 1-10 are physical indicators and questions 11-20 are behavioral indicators.

1. I get a knot in my stomach before an exam.	
2. I feel nauseous before an exam.	
3. I get sweaty palms before an exam.	
4. I feel shaky before an exam.	
5. I have trouble sleeping the night before a test.	
6. My heart rate is increased before a test.	
7. I get pains in my neck and back prior to an exam.	
8. I lose my appetite before a test.	
9. I get headaches before a test.	
10. I feel fatigued before a test.	
11. I answer questions too fast.	
12. I make careless mistakes.	
13. I can't focus during the exam; my mind wanders.	
14. During the exam, I can't recall information I thought I knew.	
15. I worry about how everybody else is doing on the exam.	
16. I have difficulty understanding the test directions.	
17. I worry about past failures while taking tests.	
18. I feel like I am running out of time on tests, even though I still finish with time left over.	
19. I feel like I studied the wrong material before the test.	
20. After a test, I suddenly remember the correct answers to questions I had difficulty with.	

If you score between a 0-10, you do not have test anxiety. If you score an 11-20, you have mild test anxiety, which can be a healthy motivator and can easily be managed. If you score 21-40, you need to be aware of how this test can affect your performance and quality of life leading up to the exam. By using the strategies presented in this guide and seeking assistance, you can overcome even the most severe anxiety. Take a few minutes to carefully think about and write down the causes of your anxiety. Then review the guide to find possible strategies to overcoming your anxiety.

In what ways do I suffer from the most anxiety?

A. _____

B. _____

C. _____

D. _____

What are some strategies to help me overcome this anxiety?

A. _____

B. _____

C. _____

D. _____

Part 1, Cognitive Assessment Sub-Areas

This is the most traditional part of the exam and contains 48 multiple choice questions, each with 4 choices (A-D). It is recommended to spend the full 2 ½ hours on this section of the exam. The questions on this section are typical of what you would expect to find on a law enforcement exam.

There are six sub areas are tested, each with eight questions in a set.

Written Comprehension: This sub-area tests for understanding and interpreting sentences and paragraphs.

Written Expression: This sub-area tests for writing words and sentences in a manner that can be understood by other people.

Problem Sensitivity: This sub-area tests for identifying when something is wrong or is about to go wrong. It includes being able to identify parts of the problem or the entire problem.

Deductive Reasoning: This sub-area tests the process of reasoning from one or more general premises to reach a logically certain conclusion.

Inductive Reasoning: Inductive reasoning is a logical process in which several pieces of information, are combined to obtain a specific conclusion.

Information Ordering: This sub-area tests for the ability to Follow set of rules or actions in a certain order. A set of rules is given. The things to be put in order can include numbers, letters, words, pictures, and procedures.

Written Comprehension

This section tests your ability to understand written language. It involves comprehension of individual words as well as sentences and paragraphs. It tests the ability to read a description of an event, understand what happened and understand the meaning of a passage. Passages are typically incident reports, policies, procedures, descriptions of events, and accident reports. These passages will be approximately 100-200 words in length and will be followed by several test questions.

Strategies for Answering Written Comprehension Questions
A. One of the most useful techniques involves is the test questions and possible answers before reading the passage. This will help you identify the information that is being sought. You may find that you locate the answer to one of the questions related to a passage before you even finish reading the passage for the first time. If so, answer the question right away. As you go from one sentence or paragraph to the next, you may have to look back at the questions to remind yourself of the details for which you are searching.

B. Another technique is to circle key words in the passage after you have read the questions. For example, if the questions related to the passage ask for information about a particular person (e.g., Mrs. Smith), then circle Mrs. Smith's name when you come to it in the passage so you don't waste time looking back through the passage later.

C. A third technique is to read for understanding without becoming bogged down by individual words you do not understand. Sometimes the meaning of a word can be decoded from the context in which it is used, or you may not need to know the definition to understand the passage. Try substituting difficult words with simpler words to help you make it through a tough passage.

D. Form a picture in your mind as you read. Visualization can be an important tool because it will help you "see" what is being written about and help you identify blanks in your understanding.

E. Ask yourself questions as you read. When you finish reading a paragraph or a long sentence, ask yourself what the passage was saying. What was the main idea of the reading? What was the author trying to say?

Sample Question

"Many of our nation's highways have evolved from older routes that were originally simple paths used by Native Americans prior to the arrival of the Europeans. Today, these roads are overused and under maintained. Most roads were never properly designed and instead have only been patched or updated when absolutely necessary. The road infrastructure today is crumbling, and the toll in deaths and injury is staggering. Today, our roads are overcrowded and dangerous."

Which one of the following statements concerning the yearly toll of traffic accidents is best supported by the passage above?
A. Higher speed is the root cause of most accidents.
B. DWI should be considered a "misdemeanor".
C. The issue does not shock us as much as it should because the accidents do not all occur together.
D. It has resulted mainly from the condition of the roads.

SOLUTION: To answer this question, evaluate all the choices.

Choice A: Nowhere in the passage does it say that speed is a cause of accidents.

Choice B: Nowhere in the passage is DWI mentioned.

Choice C: The passage does not speak specifically to "shocking" us, nor does it mention the timing of the accidents.

Choice D: This passage is about the poor condition of the roads and their relationship to accidents.

Answer: D.

Written Comprehension Question Set

Directions: After reading the selection below, choose the alternative which best answers the question following the selection.

The person in custody must, prior to interrogation, be clearly informed that he has the right to remain silent, and that anything he says will be used against him in court; he must be clearly informed that he has the right to consult with a lawyer and to have the lawyer with him during interrogation, and that, if he is indigent, a lawyer will be appointed to represent him.

-Justice Earl Warren, Miranda vs. Arizona.

1. Which one of the following best describes what must happen before a person in custody is interrogated?
A. He must remain silent.
B. He must be clearly informed of his right to remain silent.
C. He must use an attorney.
D. An attorney will be freely assigned to him in all circumstances.

Directions: After reading the selection below, choose the alternative which best answers the question following the selection.

The County Clerk generally forwards all mail to the judge in his or her county. But, the addresses of Supreme Court Clerks are also included for your convenience. If you are unsure of the Supreme Court address, always send your mail to the County Clerk, who will forward it to the appropriate party.
If you already have an index number, you should send your documentation to the Supreme Court Clerk and should include the index number with all correspondence. If you do not have an index number and you are filing a new petition (like an Article 52

petition), you need to file a Request for Judicial Intervention ("RJI") with the County Clerk to obtain an index number. When mailing documentation, you should make specific reference to the person you are trying to contact.

2. Based on the above passage, which of the following statements is most accurate?
A. It is the County Clerk's responsibility to forward all mail to the Judge in his or her county.
B. County Clerks should read all of the judge's mail.
C. County Clerks may respond on behalf of a judge.
D. A Clerk must return all mail not sent directly to a specific Judge.

3. According to the passage, why is the address of the Supreme Court Clerk provided?
A. It makes things easier for the Clerk.
B. for the convenience of the County Clerk.
C. for the convenience of the reader.
D. to expedite the filing of the documents.

4. If you are unsure of the Supreme Court address, always
A. send it to the postmaster.
B. hire a courier.
C. send it return receipt.
D. send it to the County Clerk.

5. If you are filing an Article 52 petition and you do not have an index number you must...
A. send it return receipt
B. request an "RJI" from the County Clerk
C. make reference to the person you are trying to contact
D. use your Social Security number

6. If you have an index number, to whom should you send your documentation?

A. Supreme Court Clerk

B. Notary Public

C. County Clerk

D. any court officer on duty

Directions: After reading the selection below, choose the alternative which best answers the questions that follow.

After commencement of an action wherein e-filing is authorized, documents may be electronically filed and served, but only by, and electronic service shall be made only upon, a party or parties who have consented thereto. A party's failure to consent to participation in electronic filing and service shall not bar any other party to the action from filing documents electronically with the County Clerk and the court or serving documents upon any other party who has consented to participation. A party who has not consented to participation shall file documents with the court and the County Clerk, and serve and be served with documents, in hard copy. When an e-filing party serves a document in hard copy on a non-participating party, the document served shall bear full signatures of all signatories and proof of such service shall be filed electronically.

7. What must happen before e-filing a document?

A. The document must be notarized

B. e-filing must be consented to by the parties being served.

C. Electronic service must be cancelled

D. All parties must be served hard copies first

8. When may a party file documents with the County Clerk electronically?
A. Only when all parties have agreed
B. Only when the County Clerk allows
C. Whenever the party chooses
D. When all parties demonstrate access to computers

9. How must a party be served papers who has not consented to electronic service?
A. Electronically, if the County Clerk allows
B. Electronically
C. In hard copy
D. Through the newspaper

10. How is proof of service filed by an e-filing party who has served papers on a party who has not consented to e-filing?
A. in person in the Clerk's Office
B. via courier
C. through the mail
D. electronically

Answers:(1.B, 2.A, 3.C, 4.D, 5.B, 6.A, 7.B, 8.C, 9.C, 10.D)

Written Expression

This question type involves using written language to communicate information or ideas to other people. These other people might include any individuals with whom the Police Officer might come in contact with such as judges, supervisors, victims, and suspects. This question type tests vocabulary, distinctions between words, grammar and the way words are ordered in sentences. Examples might include explaining the reason for a traffic summons to a motorist, the process of an arrest to a perpetrator, or the description of an accident to a commanding officer.

For these questions, it is important that the answer correctly conveys the content of the original idea and also expresses the idea in a clear manner. While reading the question, ask yourself: "What is the best way to say this".
The best way to prepare for this type of question is to practice writing short paragraphs that explain an idea or procedure.

Tips to help you improve your verbal expression skills:
- Think of your task during this part of the exam as being a proofreader or editor. Read slowly and thoughtfully. One strategy is to read the paragraph backwards. This is particularly helpful for checking spelling. Start with the last word on the paragraph and work your way back to the beginning, reading each word separately. Because the content or grammar won't make any sense, your focus will be on the spelling of each word.
- Separate the text into individual sentences. This will help you to read every sentence carefully. Read each sentence separately, looking for grammar, punctuation, or content errors.
- Notice each punctuation mark. As you examine each one, ask yourself "is this punctuation correct?"
- Read slowly, and read every word. Try mouthing the words without making any noise. This forces you to think about each word and how the words work together. When you

read too fast, you will skip over errors.

- Make a point of reading every day. As you read, frequently stop and try to mentally put the information you are reading into your own words. Try to verbally restate what you have read. As you read, practice locating the subjects and verbs of various sentences. Try to determine why a certain verb is required to complement a particular kind of subject.

- As you read, make a list of unfamiliar words. Afterwards, look up these words in the dictionary and write down their definitions in a notebook. By writing down these words and their definitions, you will be able to remember them more easily.

- Study and learn the words in the glossary found in the back of the book. Many of the terms are found on the exam. Having a strong familiarity with these terms will increase your confidence level.

Sample Question

NOTES: Responded to a call from 1325 Mockingbird Lane. Residence of Francine and Zachary Taylor. Parked in front of house. Saw a man on the Taylors' porch. Identified himself as Mr. Johnson, a neighbor.

QUESTION: Which one of the following choices most clearly and accurately expresses the facts presented in the notes?

A. I responded to a call from 1325 Mockingbird Lane, the residence of Francine and Zachary Taylor. When I parked in front of the house, I saw a man on their porch. He identified himself as Mr. Johnson, a neighbor.

B. Responding to a call from 1325 Mockingbird Lane, the residence of Francine and Zachary Taylor, and parking on the street in front of the house, I saw a neighbor on their porch, who identified himself as Mr. Johnson.

C. When I responded to a call from 1325 Mockingbird Lane, the residence of Francine and Zachary Taylor, I saw parking on the street in front of their house a man on their porch who identified himself as Mr. Johnson, a neighbor.

D. Responding to a call from 1325 Mockingbird Lane, I saw a man on the porch of Francine and Zachary Taylor's residence. He identified himself as Mr. Johnson's neighbor.

SOLUTION:

Choice A: This choice presents all the information in the notes in the correct sequence. This choice states that the officer responded to a call from the Taylor residence, parked on the street in front of the house, and saw man on their porch who identified himself as Mr. Johnson, a neighbor.

Choice B: "I saw a neighbor on their porch" suggests that the officer knew that it was a neighbor on the porch before Mr. Johnson told the officer who he was. This choice is incorrect.

Choice C: This response is not phrased and punctuated correctly. This choice is incorrect.

Choice D: This choice does not identify 1325 Mockingbird Lane as the residence of Francine and Zachary Taylor. Also, another piece of information is missing: the officer does not write that he parked in front of the house. This choice is incorrect.

The correct answer is A.

Written Expression Question Set

Directions: The passages below each contains five numbered blanks. Read the passage once quickly to get the overall idea of the passage. Read it a second time, this time thinking of words that might fit in the blanks. Below the passage are listed sets of words numbered to match the blanks. Pick the word from each set which seems to make the most sense both in the sentence and the total paragraph.

The Secretary of State___(1)___ the county clerk of the county ___(2)___ which the commission of a notary public is filed may certify to the official character of ___(3)___ notary public and any notary public may file his autograph signature and a certificate of official character in the office of ___(4)___ county clerk of any county in the ___(5)___ and in any register's office in any county having a register and thereafter such county clerk may certify as to the official character of such notary public.

Question 1	Question 2	Question 3	Question 4	Question 5
A. that	A. in	A. all	A. any	A. State
B. of	B. at	B. many	B. all	B. town
C. your	C. for	C. such	C. none	C. village
D. or	D. to	D. all	D. neither	D. hamlet

Answers: (1.D, 2. A, 3.C, 4.A, 5.A)

The world is (1) different now. For man holds (2) his mortal hands the power to (3) all forms of human poverty and all forms of human life. And yet the same revolutionary (4) for which our forebears fought are still at issue around the globe — the belief that the rights of man come not (5) the generosity of the state, but from the hand of God.

John F. Kennedy's Inaugural Address

Question 1	Question 2	Question 3	Question 4	Question 5
A. that	A. at	A. abolish	A. beliefs	A. where
B. another	B. for	B. tell	B. kind	B. from
C. very	C. in	C. believe	C. reason	C. whether
D. a	D. behind	D. suggest	D. offer	D. with

Answers: (1. C, 2. C, 3. A, 4. A, 5.B)

When in the course of human events (1) becomes necessary for one people to dissolve the political bands which have connected them (2) another and to assume (3) the powers of the earth, the separate and equal station to which the (4) of Nature and of Nature's God entitle them, a decent respect to the opinions (5) mankind requires that they should declare the causes which impel them to the separation.

- Declaration of Independence

Question 1	Question 2	Question 3	Question 4	Question 5
A. that	A. at	A. abolish	A. beliefs	A. of
B. another	B. with	B. among	B. Laws	B. from
C. it	C. in	C. believe	C. reason	C. whether
D. a	D. behind	D. suggest	D. offer	D. with

Answers: (1. C, 2. B, 3.B, 4. B, 5.A)

Identifying Errors in Sentences
Read through each sentence and identify the error. If there is no error, select choice E, "no error".

1. The recruits <u>have learned</u> that <u>they</u> can handle problems more effectively <u>through</u> active listening <u>and not</u> through a show of force.
A. have learned
B. they
C. through
D. and not
E. no error

2. <u>After</u> hours of physical training, the commander has decided <u>to suspend</u> further training <u>of the recruit</u> until <u>their</u> next session.
A. After
B. to suspend
C. of the recruit
D. their
E. no error

3. At the graduation ceremony, Henry <u>enjoyed listening</u> to the commissioner's insightful message, <u>which he</u> thought was <u>more sophisticated</u> <u>than the other speakers</u>.
A. enjoyed listening
B. which he
C. more sophisticated
D. than the other speakers
E. no error.

4. Originally a <u>protest against</u> <u>stop and frisk policies</u>, the Innocence project <u>exerted</u> great influence on policing <u>of its</u> time.

A. protest against

B. stop and frisk policies

C. exerted

D. of its

E. no error

5. <u>The officers</u> <u>made an</u> amazing arrest <u>when he</u> took <u>in three</u> bank robbery suspects.

A. The officers

B. made an

C. when he

D. in three

E. no error

6. The <u>car ignored</u> the stop sign <u>and proceeded</u> to cross the intersection <u>and crash</u> <u>into a</u> parked garbage truck.

A. car ignored

B. and proceeded

C. and crash

D. into a

E. no error

7. The perpetrator ran <u>through the</u> courtyard <u>and across</u> the park <u>until they</u> collapsed <u>from exhaustion</u>.

A. through the

B. and across

C. until they

D. from exhaustion

E. no error

8. A weapon <u>must be</u> handled <u>with cares</u> and respect <u>at all</u> times. The <u>use of</u> a deadly weapon is not to be taken lightly.

A. must be

B. with cares

C. at all

D. use of

E. No Error

Answers: (1. D, 2. D, 3. D 4. E, 5. C, 6. A, 7.C, 8. B)

Problem Sensitivity

This is the ability to recognize and identify problems. It involves both the recognition of the problem as a whole and the parts of the problem. You will not be expected to solve the problem, only to identify or recognize it.

Examples of this ability are recognizing when to stop and question a group of individuals; treat an injured person; wait for medical assistance; radio information about roadway conditions; or report a mechanical issue with a squad car. This ability would also involve recognizing an explanation that someone provides in a particular situation that is diversionary.

Strategies for Problem Sensitivity Questions
There are two types of questions that you may encounter. The first type will begin with the presentation of some rules, procedures, or recommended practices followed by the description of a situation in which these rules should be applied. Based on the applicable rules, you will be required to identify a problem (or the most serious of several problems) with the way the incident was handled. Because this first type of problem sensitivity question typically involves the presentation of a large amount of initial information, many of the suggested strategies for verbal comprehension questions (e.g., underlining key information) will assist you with these types of questions.

The second type of question will consist of stories by victims and witnesses. For these questions, a problem exists when a witness gives information that is different from information supplied by other witnesses.

Problem Sensitivity Sample Question Type A:
A police officer may have to use his or her patrol vehicle on a roadway to warn drivers of a hazardous road condition by blocking the hazard and activating the flashing light bar.
For which one of the following situations should an officer block the roadway?
A. A 4-lane road with no emergency phone.
B. A narrow 2-lane road with an obstruction in the middle.
C. A road recently repaved.
D. A road covered with dry leaves.

Correct Answer: B.

Problem Sensitivity Sample Question Type B:
A police officer may be called upon to help settle disputes. Which one of the following situations should the officer help settle?
A. Two men talking about sports outside a bar.
B. A mechanic arguing with a customer about an unpaid repair.
C. Four senior citizens discussing workout schedules with a gym manager.
D. A man and a woman running having a discussion about their child's school.

Correct Answer: B. It is the only choice that indicates some type of conflict. Conflict can lead to violence.

Problem Sensitivity Practice Set

1. Officer Francis interviewed four witnesses to an accident that took place at the intersection of 4th and Main. They described the accident as follows:

Witness 1 - "The white station wagon blew the stop sign and T-boned the minivan."

Witness 2 - "The white car just kept going. He didn't slow down and hit that family in the van. The van made a complete stop and then the other guy hit them."

Witness 3 - "The guy in the white car was on his phone. He didn't even see the stop sign."

Witness 4 - "I was following my friend in the Audi station wagon. Of course he stopped. He looked both ways. He is a very careful driver. I don't know what the other driver said, but it cannot be my friend's fault".

According to the information provided, Officer Francis should recognize that there is a problem with the account given by witness:

A. Witness 1.
B. Witness 2.
C. Witness 3.
D. Witness 4.

2. Use the information in the following passage to answer this question:

Law Enforcement Agencies have standard procedures in place for handling calls for hostage situations:

I. Certified dispatchers attempt to keep the caller talking and work to obtain as much information possible, while working to calm the caller.

II. No attempt is made to enter the premises where the call is coming from until all units are in place and a command post is set up.

III. The decision to evacuate a building or surrounding homes is made by the commanding officer once the command post is established and personnel are in place.

IV. No public statements are to be made to the media by police until the scene is secure.

V. If one perpetrator commits violence, there is always the possibility of additional perpetrators nearby targeting law enforcement personnel. In this regard, every effort should be made to maintain a secure perimeter, and a room by room, house by house search can be made. Once the all clear signal is given, residents can resume their occupancy of the premises.

According to the preceding passage, of the four actions described below, the potentially most serious error would occur if:

A. Immediately after a hostage shooting, Sargent Thomas began shooting blindly into the house.

B. While standing by at the scene of a hostage situation, probationary officer Jones provided information regarding the incident to a reporter.

C. While standing by at the scene of a hostage situation, Officer Smith told onlookers to move back to a safe distance.

D. After hostage situation ended and the all clear signal was given Captain Rodriguez informed the apartment building manager to allow residents back into the building.

3. Officer Francis is patrolling a neighborhood around 7:30 a.m. when he notices a car that is missing a rear license plate and has a loud exhaust. He pulls the car over for a traffic stop. As he steps out of the police car, the driver of the car steps out of her vehicle and walks towards him with what appears to be receipts for automotive repairs.

Before Officer Francis can say a word, the driver apologizes for the loud exhaust and explains that she had just paid a mechanic a great sum of money. She shows Officer Francis her driver's license and says that she hopes that the situation can be taken care of quickly. The woman seems frustrated and upset; she does not smell of alcohol, and she walks straight, without swaying. Officer Francis orders the woman to go back inside her car. He adds that he will also need to see proof of insurance. The woman hesitates to return to the vehicle. Officer Francis again orders the woman to return to her car. The woman states, "This isn't necessary, I am not doing anything wrong. I need to get to work or I'll be fired". Officer Francis must order her to return to her car a third time before she complies.

Based on the above information, what, if anything, is most likely to be the woman's problem?
A) The woman is just impatient to return to work.
B) The woman has something in his car that he does not want Officer Francis to see.
C) The woman is under the influence of alcohol.
D) The woman is nervous because she has no insurance, registration, or inspection and fears a ticket.

4. Officer Harley noticed a teenage girl wearing a heavyweight coat sleeping in a bus shelter at 4:30 AM. Officer Harley approached the girl and asked if everything was okay. The girl stated that everything was OK, but that she was hungry. Officer Harley noticed that the girl had what appeared to be cigarette burns on her arms. She asked the girl how she received the burns, and the girl quietly replied that she had been injured baking cookies. Officer Harley was not convinced that burns were caused in the way described by the girl.
Based on the passage above, what information should Officer Harley use as evidence of the girl's injuries?
A. The information regarding the girl's baking.
B. The fact that a woman reported seeing the girl.
C. The fact that the girl was wearing a heavy coat.
D. The fact that the girl did not give a plausible explanation for the injuries and got quiet when discussing their cause.

5. Imagine that you are an officer assigned to central booking. Which of the following problems would you investigate FIRST?
A. A prisoner complains that another detainee in the vicinity is repeatedly humming loudly, interrupting everybody's sleep.
B. A prisoner repeatedly curses to himself.
C. A prisoner is complaining of being thirsty.
D. A prisoner informs you that another detainee in the holding area has passed out and is foaming at the mouth.

6. A police officer responds to the scene of an accident. Four people are injured. Which person does the officer tend to first?
A. A 24-year old man complaining of a sore hand
B. A 7-month old baby who is blue and appears to be choking
C. A 7-year-old girl who is alert but crying
D. A 54-year-old woman who is complaining that she bumped her head, but who is and alert and talking clearly

7. Which scene appears to be a potential problem?
A. Two women having coffee at a sidewalk café
B. 3 teenagers playing basketball in a park
C. A store owner arguing with a delivery man over an unpaid bill
D. a man walking his dog on a leash

8. Four calls come into dispatch at the same time. Which call is the highest priority?
A. A report of a loud stereo at 10:01 on a Saturday night
B. The report of a lost dog
C. A homeowner reporting that a bicycle was stolen some time ago.
D. A report of an accident involving a school bus and a chemical truck

9. A law enforcement officer has the right to search lost or abandoned property for the purpose of ensuring public safety and attempting to locate and return property to its rightful owner. Which scenario would empower an officer to search property?
A. A pocketbook found alone on a park bench with no owner visible
B. A car parked overnight at the municipal parking garage
C. The garage of a known drug dealer
D. A vacation home that is not currently occupied

10. You are a police officer. At roll call, your commanding officer gives you instructions that are unclear to you. What should you do?
 A. You should respectfully ask the commanding officer to repeat the unclear instructions.
B. You should call your friend, a retired captain for assistance.
C. Follow only the parts of the instructions that you understand, and ignore the rest.
D. Complete the task as best as you can and then check with the commanding officer if the task was done correctly.

11. **Rule:** According to the police department rules, officers will NOT make comments to the press or make notification to the relatives of an officer who is killed or injured while on duty without the permission of the commanding officer.

Situation: An officer from the 3rd Precinct was seriously injured in an automobile accident while chasing a robbery suspect. Upon precinct, police officer Thompson received a call from Police Officer Washington's wife, asking to speak to officer Washington, Officer Thompson informed her that officer Washington was at the hospital because he got injured while chasing a suspect.
Officer Thompson's action was:
A. Proper, because officer Washington's wife asked for him.
B. Proper, because the family always should be notified as soon as possible in cases of serious injury or death.
C. Improper, because officer Thompson did not have the authority to make such a notification.
D. Improper, because this kind of notification should be done in person.

Police officers are required to use handcuffs to secure prisoners. When officers are using handcuffs, what action would pose a threat to the prisoner in custody?
A. Protecting the prisoner's head when placing them in a squad car
B. Using a seat belt to ensure the prisoner is safe while driving
C. Tightening the handcuffs, so they cut off circulation
D. Checking the hands often for discoloration or irritation

Answers:
(1. D, 2. A, 3. D, 4. D, 5. D, 6. B, 7. C, 8. D, 9. A, 10. A, 11. C)

Deductive Reasoning

Deductive reasoning begins with a general fact and creates a specific conclusion from that generalization. This is the opposite of inductive reasoning, which involves creating broad generalizations from specific observations. The basic idea of deductive reasoning is that if something is true of a group of things, this truth applies to all members of that group. One of the keys for successful deductive reasoning, then, is to be able to correctly identify members of the group, because incorrect categorizations will result in incorrect conclusions. For deductive reasoning to work, the original fact set must also must be correct. If the original set of facts is wrong, even if the logic used is correct, the answer will still be wrong.

You can better understand deductive reasoning by looking at an example. A generalization might be something such as, "Every octopus has eight arms." A logical conclusion for this example is, "This is an octopus, so it must have eight arms." This is a valid deduction. The validity of the deduction, however, depends on whether the creature is actually an octopus. A common error in this logic would be to say, "This creature has eight arms, so it must be an octopus".

On the exam, you will be asked how to apply general rules to particular cases. There are two different types of deductive reasoning questions which appear on law enforcement exams:

1. Applying rules and procedures to particular situations
2. Applying legal definitions to the facts of particular situations.

Applying Rules and Procedures

In constructing law enforcement exams, test makers treat department rules and procedures as general principles which must be applied in the circumstances of particular situations. Questions based on rules or procedures begin with a statement of the department rule or procedure. For example, the question could state the procedure for signing in before roll call. The question might then give a description of an officer arriving to work late. The question will then ask about how the officer should go about signing in.

When answering these questions, do not think about your own experience. You may be familiar with the policy or procedure being tested. Do not let this cloud your reasoning. Everything you need to know to answer the question is contained in the policy or procedure provided.

Rules and procedures assure that laws are enforced fairly and equally, allow for a chain of command to operate, and enhance the ability of various law enforcement and public safety agencies to coordinate a response to an emergency. These questions are designed to test your ability to follow and apply rules. There will not be any "trick" psychological questions in this part.

Here are some strategies for answering deductive reasoning questions:

1. Follow the steps of a procedure in order.

2. Pay attention to when the rule is in effect.

3. Pay attention to when the rule is not in effect.

4. Identify when there are exemptions to a rule and know when to apply the exemption. The key words to help you identify an exemption are "unless", "except", "when", and "if".

5. If a rule or procedure has several parts, make sure the answer satisfies all of the parts. When answering this type of question, it is important for you to reread the question and ask yourself, "is there anything missing from this answer?"

6. In choosing an answer, apply rules exactly as written. Remember, this is an exam for an entry level position in law enforcement. The exam is testing how well you follow directions and carry out orders, not how well you interpret vague philosophy.

Here is a list of some basic standard operating procedures common to most law enforcement agencies. Use this only as a guide to become familiar with rules. When taking the exam, rely only on the information provided in the question.

Confidentiality

Officers shall treat the official business of the department as confidential. Officers shall not release information concerning the name or condition of accident or crime victims.

Contact with The Public

Officers shall be courteous and civil when dealing with the public. Any conduct to the contrary shall not be tolerated.

Department Property

Officers shall be responsible for the good care of all property assigned to them and shall report to their commanding officer any loss, damage to or unserviceable condition of such property.

False Information

No Officer shall complete any report using false and inaccurate information.

Gratuities

Officers shall not seek free admission for themselves or others to theaters of other places of amusements. Officers shall not receive money, gifts, gratuities, food or beverages, rewards or compensation for police services rendered.

Identification

Officers shall give all proper information to persons requesting it in a careful, courteous and accurate manner. Officers shall give their names and badge number in a respectful manner to any person who may request the information.

Investigation

Officers shall investigate all cases of injury to persons or damage to property to any public place which may come to their attention.

Orders

Officers shall promptly obey any lawful orders given by any officer of higher rank.

Patrol Area

Officers shall not leave their assigned area unless directly ordered by their supervisors, are sent to another area by the dispatcher or for other emergencies.

Statements

No member shall speak on behalf of the department unless authorized to do so by the police commissioner.

Substance Use

Officers shall not consume any intoxicating liquors while on duty. Officers shall not take any medication, prescribed or otherwise unless approved to do so by the medical bureau.

Timeliness

Officers shall be punctual in reporting for duty at the time designated by the department.

Traffic Enforcement

All members of the department are responsible for the enforcement of traffic laws regardless of their duty assignment.

Uniform

Officers shall be in complete uniform when on duty. No mixture of civilian and uniform clothing shall be permitted in public, or off-duty.

Applying Legal Definitions:

This exam requires the candidate to apply laws to situations. The test-taker is not expected to know any of the laws. The laws are stated as part of the question. These questions look like reading comprehension questions, but they are designed to test the candidate's ability to reason based on legal definitions and apply them to specific situations. These questions provide the definitions for several different classes of crimes. The definitions are oversimplified. Your task for answering this type of question is to answer solely on the definition provided and <u>not from your own background knowledge</u>.

After providing several definitions, the questions describe a specific situation. The candidate is then asked what type of crime, if any, was committed and who committed it.

These questions require you to pay careful attention to detail. You can count on there being answer choices that are in place to catch up a careless or fast reader.

The definition of a crime will have several parts, all of which must be present for a crime to have taken place. If any one of the parts is missing, then the particular crime could not have been committed.

Try to break the definition down into its parts. Make a mental checklist. In order for the crime to have been committed, all parts of the checklist must be satisfied.

While reading a legal definition, be on the lookout for important punctuation marks like colons or semicolons that may be indicators of the separate parts of a definition. Also watch out for the conjunctions "and" and "or". Use of the word "and", means that two or more parts must have occurred for a crime to have been committed. If the word "or" is used, then only one part out of many is necessary for the crime to have been committed.

Strategies for answering Deductive Reasoning Questions:

1. Read carefully. There are false choices designed to fool a careless reader.

2. Make sure the choice matches all parts of a rule, policy, or definition.

3. Use only the information provided. Do not rely on your own knowledge of an actual rule or definition.

4. Keep in mind that these questions are meant to test your ability to follow directions. Your job is not to interpret how correct a policy or definition is.

Sample Question Applying Rules and Procedures

RULE: Patrol vehicles should be inspected immediately prior to the start of each shift. Do not assume that the vehicle is in safe working condition. Check that all of the lighting is operational, all emergency equipment is present, operate the siren, check engine, oil level, engine coolant level, gasoline level, tire pressure and condition, spare tire, lug wrench, jack, windshield wipers and windshield washer fluid level. Check the body of the vehicle for damaged or missing parts and report any damage or malfunction to your sergeant. At the end of your shift, leave the vehicle in safe operational condition for use by the next officer.

SITUATION: Officer Davis is about to begin his patrol shift when he discovers that his police vehicle has a large scratch and dent in the right rear quarter panel. He knows that the vehicle did not have this dent yesterday, when he last drove it.

QUESTION: According to the above Rule, Officer Davis should most properly

    A. request that he be assigned a different vehicle

    B. begin his shift and be alert to any operating problems

    C. find out what other officers have used the vehicle since his last shift

    D. inform his sergeant about the dented bumper

SOLUTION: The situation states that Officer Davis has discovered a dent in the quarter panel of his patrol vehicle that did not exist when he last used it. The question asks what he should do about it. To answer the question, evaluate all of the choices.

Choice A states that the officer should request a different vehicle. There is nothing in the rule that states that the officer should do this. Choice A is incorrect.

Choice B states that the officer should begin his shift and be alert to any operating problems. The rule states that the officer should report any problems with the vehicle to his supervisor. Choice B is correct.

Choice C states that the officer should find out what other officers have used the vehicle since his last shift. There is nothing in the rule that states that the officer should do this. Choice C is incorrect.

Choice D states that the officer should inform his supervisor about the damaged quarter panel. This conforms to the given rule that states that the officer should report any problems, damage, or discrepancies to her supervisor. Choice D is the correct answer.

The answer is D.

Rule Relating to Leaves of Absence

Prepare a Leave of Absence Report and submit it to commanding the officer for approval, at least five days before leave commences except in emergency.

2. Leaves may be terminated at discretion of police commissioner.

3. A member who is granted an extended leave of absence without pay must take all accrued leave prior to the start of the leave of absence, except for military leave.

4. Leave without pay for thirty (30) or more consecutive days during a year, except military leave, will reduce authorized vacation by one twelfth for each thirty (30) consecutive days of absence.

5. Am ember returning from leave without pay for one (1) year or more may not be granted un-accrued vacation until member performs active duty for a minimum of three (3) months, unless otherwise authorized by law.

6. A member of the service (uniformed or civilian) applying for any extended leave, e.g., educational leave with or without pay, hardship leave, etc., is required to communicate with the Military and Extended Leave Desk for instructions.

7. Leave without pay may be granted to observe a religious holiday. No more than sixth of each squad may be granted such leave.

Questions:

1. If a police officer has a documented family emergency and desires to submit for a leave of absence, what must he or she do?
A. wait five days and then submit the paperwork.
B. go to family and apply after the fact.
C. submit paperwork immediately requesting immediate leave.
D. submit paperwork and wait the required 5 days.

2. If a police officer has been approved for a leave for educational purposes and an emergency strikes the Municipality, who has the power to terminate Leaves of Absence?
A. the police commissioner
B. each commanding officer
C. the Mayor
D. No one. The leave was already granted.

3. If a member is called up for military service,
A. he must first use up all of his accrued leave time.
B. he does not have to use his accrued leave time.
C. he must not go.
D. he must wait until a replacement is found.

4. A member goes on leave without pay for 31 days. She has accrued 12 vacation days. How many days will be deducted?
A. 12
B. 6
C. 3
D. 1

5. A member returns from a two your leave of absence. How long must he or she wait until applying for a vacation?
A. Immediately
B. 1 month
C. 3 months
D. 1 year

6. A member desires to take a leave of absence to attend law school at Brooklyn Law. With whom must the member communicate?
A. desk sergeant
B. commanding officer
C. Internal Investigations desk
D. Military and Extended Leaves Desk

7. A squad has 60 members. The Easter religious holiday is approaching. How many members may be granted an unpaid leave of absence from the squad?
A. None B. 6   C. 10   D. 60

Answers: (1. C, 2. A, 3. B, 4. D, 5. C, 6. D, 7. C)

Procedures for utilizing the information system

Purpose: to inform members of the service of the guidelines to be complied with when accessing, creating, receiving, disclosing or otherwise maintaining information from an information system.

1. Access only those information systems to which authorization has been granted and under circumstances required in the execution of lawful duty.

2. Abide by any security terms/conditions associated with the information system, including those governing user passwords, and logon procedures. All users must log out any time they leave the terminal.

3. No not disclose information to others, including other service members, only as required in the execution of lawful duty.

4. Confirm identity and affiliation of requestor of information and determine that release of information is lawful, prior to disclosure.

5. Maintain confidentiality of information accessed, created, received, disclosed or otherwise maintained during course of duty.

Questions:

1. If an officer desires to use the system, when is it permissible to borrow another officer's password?

A. during off-duty hours
B. during regular shift
C. never. Access is not authorized
D. only with cooperating officer present

2. An officer is using the information system terminal and feels the urge to use the restroom. The officer should

A. logoff
B. turn off screen
C. Ask sergeant to watch computer
D. leave it on, as it will take too long to reboot

3. An officer has a friend that works for a local newspaper. The friend requests information from the officer. What should the officer do?
A. arrest the friend
B. refer the friend to the office of media relations
C. allow the friend to only view the material, not print it
D. print the information the friend requested

4. What should an officer do if someone calls on the precinct phone and states that they are with the FBI and need information on a "perp".
A. offer to give the information
B. hang up
C. refer the caller to the commanding officer for verification of credentials
D. take down the caller's information and then give them the requested information.

Answers: (1. C, 2. A, 3. B, 4. C)

UNIFORMS

1. Maintain at own expense articles prescribed for rank, position or duty. *Recruits wear uniform only after inspected and stamped by police academy.*

2. Do not modify prescribed uniforms in any manner except as specifically authorized by higher authority.

3. Do not wear distinguishable items of the uniform with civilian clothes.

4. Do not wear uniform, shield or display **IDENTIFICATION CARD** while participating in a rally, demonstration or other public assemblage except as authorized by the department.

5. Wear uniform of the day. Commanding officers or unit commanders may authorize a specialized uniform only after requesting and receiving approval from the police commissioner's Uniform and Equipment Review Committee. Submit requests to the Office of the Chief of Department: Attn: Uniform and Equipment Sub-Committee.

a. Wear uniform when directed, if assigned to the Detective Bureau or to duty in civilian clothes.

6. While performing duty indoors, in uniform, wear regulation seasonal shirt and trousers.

7. Wear the prescribed uniform, if regularly assigned to duty in uniform, when appearing in court, the trial room or at the office of a ranking officer above the rank of captain, except if off duty, on sick report, or if excused by competent authority.

8. Purchase regulation service holsters, caps, raingear and all items of uniform which are sewn or attached to the uniform, from the equipment section or other authorized supplier.

9. Necessary uniform changes, other than those listed in step 10, will be made as directed by the lieutenant platoon commander/counterpart.

a. The lieutenant platoon commander/counterpart shall authorize the removal, if desired, of the duty jacket/summer blouse whenever the temperature for a **specific** tour is expected to rise above 65 degrees Fahrenheit.

b. The lieutenant platoon commander/counterpart shall authorize the wearing of the **optional** short sleeve shirt whenever the temperature for a **specific** tour is expected to rise above 70 degrees Fahrenheit.

Questions:

1. An officer desires to replace uniform articles. He or she must…
A. submit a voucher for payment from the department
B. request the new articles from the quartermaster at 1 Police Plaza
C. pay for the articles from an authorized vendor
D. wait until the annual uniform fund is established

2. An officer desires to place a small gold cross on the left collar of the uniform. Who may authorize such an alteration?
A. the Commissioner's Uniform and Equipment Review Committee
B. the union
C. the officer's clergy
D. fellow officers

3. An officer desires to attend an immigration rally. They must…
A. hand in their gun and shield
B. not wear their shield or ID card
C. not attend any rally
D. may proudly display badge as long as Class A uniform is worn

4. When appearing in court, officers should wear…
A. street clothes
B. regular uniform
C. suit and tie for men, dress and blouse for ladies
D. former military uniform if ever in service

5. From who may an officer purchase a holster?
A. any sporting goods store
B. from an authorized retailer
C. from police academy
D. from retired officer

6. The temperature is expected to rise to 68 degrees Fahrenheit for a specific tour. The Lieutenant may authorize…
A. shorts
B. removal of duty jacket or summer blouse
C. street clothes
D. sneakers, socks, and athletic wear

7. The temperature is expected to rise to 80 degrees Fahrenheit. The lieutenant may authorize the use of...
A. shorts
B. short- sleeved shirt
C. sneakers
D. street clothes

Answers: (1. C, 2. A, 3. B, 4. B, 5. B, 6. B, 7. B)

Rule

The Counterterrorism Bureau recently distributed personal protective equipment to over 30,000 uniformed members of the service. This equipment is designed to enhance the personal safety of uniformed members in the event of a disaster or catastrophic incident, including those of a chemical or biological nature. Included in the personal protective kit is a tactical response hood contained in a cloth carry pouch. This item is designed to be attached to the gun belt worn by uniformed members. As such, it should be carried by, and available to, all uniformed members performing patrol duty in uniform.

Members are reminded that the tactical response hood is designed for a single escape of up to 15 minutes from a contaminated area. They do not provide oxygen and are not intended for use in an oxygen-deprived environment.

2. Therefore, effective immediately, uniformed members of the service will carry the tactical response hood as follows:

a. Members performing patrol duties in a department vehicle will have the hood and pouch available in the vehicle;

b. Members performing foot patrol duties and/or assigned to a detail such as a parade, fixed post, etc. will carry the tactical response hood by attaching the pouch to their gun belts on the side opposite which the member carries his/her firearm;

c. Members performing administrative or other duties inside a department facility will have the tactical response hood and pouch readily available at all times.

3. The balance of the personal protective equipment issued to uniformed members of the service will be carried in department vehicles by those members of the service performing patrol duties in such vehicles. All other uniformed members of the service will have the balance of the personal protective equipment readily available, e.g. stored in their department locker.

4. Any provisions of the Department Manual or other department directive in conflict with the contents of this order are suspended.

Questions:

1. An officer is on car patrol at night in northern Queens, she should…
A. wear the personal protective equipment
B. carry the personal protective equipment on the gun belt on opposite side from weapon
C. give the personal protective equipment to family
D. leave the personal protective equipment in the trunk of the squad car

2. In the event of a chemical attack, the hood is designed to protect an officer …
A. for a shift
B. for 15 minutes
C. for 1 hour
D. indefinitely

3. An officer is assigned to foot patrol along the Steuben Day Parade. Where should the officer keep the personal protective gear?
A. in a backpack
B. in the precinct
C. at the command post
D. on their gun belt

4. A member is assigned to light duty at the precinct following an automobile accident while on duty. The officer
A. must wear their personal protective device on his/her gun belt
B. must keep the personal protective device in his/her locker
C. does not need the personal protective device
D. must keep the personal protective device close at hand

Answers: (1. B, 2. B, 3. D, 4. D)

Inductive Reasoning

This type of question combines separate pieces of data to form general conclusions. It requires the ability to formulate possible reasons for why things fit together.

You will be asked to make general conclusions based on the information provided in tables, charts, and graphs. Most inductive reasoning questions will start with a passage which provides you the information you will need to answer the question. Scan the passage to determine the main idea, and then read the questions. The questions will ask you to identify similarities and differences within the reading. You can expect to be asked to identify trends and patterns and to predict future results based on given set of data.

How Improve your Inductive Reasoning Skills:
Be sure to carefully read every part of the question. Carefully examine all charts, graphs, and sub-text. If you misread a number or a variable, you will not be able to find the correct answer. Modern exams account for this by providing wrong answer choices that match a hastily made conclusion.

You can prepare for inductive reasoning questions by looking through a newspaper or a magazine for a chart or graph. Before reading the article or advertisement that accompanies the graph, try making interpretations and drawing conclusions about the data. Then read the article to see if your conclusions match the analysis given by the text.

Many advertisements use graphs to "spin" their product. Try to identify ways that a graph or chart is misleading. Analyze charts and graphs for missing information that change the graphic's meaning.

Sample Question

During a simulation exercise, recruits at the Academy learn that as officers, they may have cause to secure scenes containing the remains of a deceased person. In this instance, an immediate notification must be made to the desk officer of the precinct, so the medical examiner can send a team to the scene. Due to the nature of the situation and the possibility that a crime has been committed, ALL members of the SCPD will follow these guidelines:

1. do Not disturb personal affects
2. DO NOT make jokes or remarks concerning the condition of the body.
3. DO NOT take pictures with the deceased
4. Use your nose. If chemical vapors are very strong or there is any odor of bitter almonds, remain outside and call for HAZ Mat response.
5. DO NOT disturb the body.
6. DO NOT talk to the press
7. DO NOT provide personal information to neighbors or onlookers.

Based on this information, it would be most correct for recruits to conclude that the primary concern behind these guidelines is:
A) proper control of evidence at a possible crime scene until a search warrant can be obtained
B) safety of the officers concerning possible explosions or exposure to fumes
C) keeping officers from accidental or intentional exposure to controlled substances (e.g. narcotics)
D) preservation of confidentiality concerning the nature of the situation

The correct answer is D.

Crime Statistics

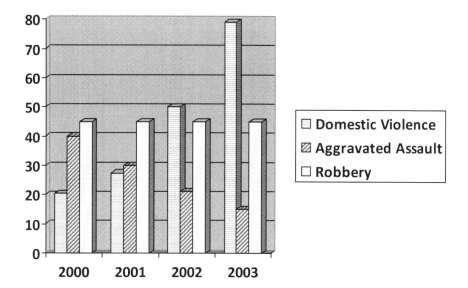

1. According to the graph, robbery
A. increased   B. fluctuated
C. decreased   D. remained the same

2. Which crime had the most instances in any given year?
A. domestic Violence   B. aggravated Assault
C. robbery   D. all were equal

3. Which crime increased each year?
A. domestic Violence   B. aggravated Assault
C. robbery   D. all remained stable

4. Which crime declined each year?
A. domestic Violence   B. aggravated Assault
C. robbery   D. all decreased each year

5. Which crime had the lowest incidents in 2002?
A. domestic Violence   B. aggravated Assault
C. robbery   D. robbery and domestic

6. Which year had the lowest crime overall?
A. 2000   B. 2002
C. 2001   D. 2003

7. If current trends continue, predict what will happen to the number of aggravated assault cases.
A. It will increase.   B. It will decrease.
C. It will remain stable.   D. It will fluctuate.

8. If current trends continue, predict what will happen to the number of domestic violence cases.
A. It will increase.   B. It will decrease.
C. It will remain stable.   D. It will fluctuate.

Answers: (1. D, 2. A, 3. A, 4. B, 5. B, 6. C, 7. B, 8. A)

Causes of Accidents 2013

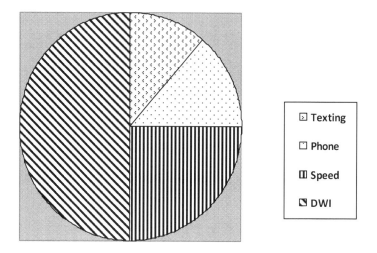

1. According to the graph, what is the greatest cause of accidents?
A. Texting   B. Phone   C. Speed   D. DWI

2. What is the approximate percentage of DWI accidents?
A. 100%   B. 75%   C. 50%   D. 25%

3. Which cause is about 25%?
A. Texting   B. Phone   C. Speed   D. DWI

4. Phones and Texting together cause as many accidents as
A. Texting and Speed   B. Phones and Speed
C. Speed   D. DWI

5. According to the graph, what is the lowest cause of accidents?
A. Texting   B. Phone   C. Speed   D. DWI

6. Which cause of accidents is greater than phone but less than DWI?

A. texting   B. phone   C. speed   D. DWI

7. Approximately what percentage do speed, texting, and phone cause combined?

A. 25%   B. 50%   C. 75%   D. 100%

8. Approximately what percentage of accidents does speed cause?

A. 25%   B. 50%   C. 75%   D. 100%

Answers: (1. D, 2. C, 3. C, 4. C, 5. A, 6. C, 7. B, 8. A)

Precinct Calls by Type and Year

	2010	2011	2012	2013
Car Accident	11	17	18	22
Auto Theft	15	21	17	19
Robbery	22	29	38	42
Petty Larceny	99	102	118	120
Total	147	169	191	203

1. According to the table, which year had the highest number of incidents?
A. 2010   B. 2011   C. 2012   D. 2013

2. According to the table, which incident happens the most often?
A. Car Accident   B. Auto Theft
C. Robbery   D. Petty Larceny

3. According to the table, which incident happens the least often?
A. Car Accident   B. Auto Theft
C. Robbery   D. Petty Larceny

4. According to the chart, precinct calls are
A. increasing   B. decreasing   C. remaining stable

5. According to the chart, which incident occurs more often than Robbery?
A. Car Accidents   B. Auto Theft
C. Petty Larceny   D. Murder

6. According to the table, which incident fluctuates?

A. Car Accident B. Auto Theft

C. Robbery D. Petty Larceny

7. According to the table, which incident occurred less than Auto Theft in 2011?

A. Car Accident B. Burglary

C. Robbery D. Petty Larceny

8. Predict which type of call will increase the least in 2014

A. Car Accident B. Auto Theft

C. Robbery D. Petty Larceny

Answers: (1. D, 2. D, 3. A, 4. A, 5. C, 6. B, 7. A, 8.B)

Information ordering

This type of question requires following a set of rules or actions in a certain order. The rules will be given. The things or actions to be put in order can include numbers, letters, words, or sentences. Questions based on information ordering measure your ability to put information into a logical order. You might be given sentences which will have to go into a paragraph, and then you are instructed to create the paragraph. You might be given a group of items and you will have to classify them. You might be asked to list things in chronological order according to time.

For information ordering questions, it is often best to come up with the answer before you look at the answer choices. After you read the information and the question, imagine the correct answer. Then look at the answer choices to find your answer.

Typically, it will be easy to determine the first and last items in the set. You can then eliminate the choices which clearly aren't correct and can then use that time to locate and verify the correct choice. Some information ordering questions will provide you with a specific procedure to follow. It is necessary to read very carefully, as the procedure will spell out exactly what you have to do. In this case, you can count on the test-makers to provide incorrect answer choices to catch careless reading. For example, if the question states that you must put the names in order of last name, first name, and middle initial, it would be an error to include the full middle name if given.

Some information ordering questions work in reverse. You will be given a procedure in the correct sequence with all of the steps outlined. You will then be asked questions about the ordering of the steps and will have to fit actions into the outlined procedure. Again, it is very important that you rely solely on the outlined procedure. Do not rely on your own experience to determine what the right order is.

The secret to success in answering information ordering questions is to be very strict in your thinking. ***Do not*** rely on outside experience.

These questions are based on the following rules:

- There is only one correct order of things.
- Every step must be followed in the correct stated order.
- No step may be missed or omitted.
- The most difficult information ordering questions include exceptions or "if", or "unless". For example, a procedure might state that an officer must use a special form if an accident she responds to will likely result in a fatality, unless the person has already been taken to a hospital. It would be an error to use the special form in all accident cases. It would also be an error to use the form if the patient has already been transported to the hospital. Therefore, it is important to take note of any time the works "if" or "unless" are used or if there are any exceptions to a procedure given.

Strategies for answering information ordering questions:

1. Follow the directions very carefully. Make sure you understand the task. Re-read the instructions until you are certain of what is being asked.

2. Locate the first step and quickly eliminate those choices which don't fit.

3. The most difficult information ordering questions contain the words "if" and "unless". Be on the lookout for any question that includes exceptions to a stated procedure.

Sample Question

Recruit officers in the academy are told that if they are in a situation in which persons are being held hostage or in which barricaded persons will not voluntarily surrender, they should do the following in the order given:

1. Notify the Communications Division of the situation, so they can notify the patrol supervisor, Emergency Service Unit, and operations unit.
2. Verify that the patrol supervisor and Emergency Service Unit are responding.
3. Attempt to confine and isolate the subjects involved, pending arrival of the patrol supervisor and Emergency Service Unit.
4. Maintain firearms control and establish police lines.
5. Maintain continuous surveillance of the location, if possible. Detain witnesses for later debriefing.

In a role-play exercise in class, the recruit officers are given a situation in which officers respond to a barricaded person situation. They have notified the Communications Division, and have verified that the patrol supervisor and the Emergency Service Unit are responding. The next step they should take is to:
A) direct the Operations Unit to respond
B) attempt to confine and isolate the subjects involved
C) maintain firearms control and establish
D) detain witnesses for later debriefing

Correct answer: B.

Information Ordering Question Set

1. Use the information in the following passage to answer the question:

When responding to an incident involving a person needing medical assistance, law enforcement officers should follow these steps in the order given:

I. Render aid to the sick or injured person

II. Request ambulance if necessary

III. Notify the dispatcher if the person is wearing a Medic-Alert bracelet or if a family member or acquaintance indicates that the person suffers from serious medical problems

IV. Wait to direct the ambulance to the scene

V. Make a second call in 15 minutes if the ambulance does not arrive

VI. Make a Log book entry, including the name of the person notified regarding the Medic-Alert emblem or statements from family acquaintance concerning the nature of the illness

While on patrol, Police Officer Humphry is approached by a man who informs the police officer that a middle aged woman was found slumped behind the steering wheel of a car. Police Officer Humphrey, while offering aid, notices that the woman is wearing a Medic-Alert emblem indicating diabetes. Police Officer Humphrey now requests an ambulance to respond. The next step the police officer should take is:

A. inform the dispatcher of the Medic-Alert emblem
B. have a responsible person direct the ambulance to the scene
C. place a second call for the ambulance after 15 minutes
D. take the woman to the hospital in the patrol car

2. Officer Stone has just finished interviewing the victim of a robbery.

The victim made the following statements:

1. When walking to the station, I saw my brother's friend, Charles Mason, standing at the entrance.

2. Charles hit me in the face and body with repeated blows with his fist.

3. I didn't want to walk past Charles because I knew he was desperate for money to buy drugs.

4. Charles grabbed my backpack and attempted to run away.

5. I ran up the stairs and escaped.

6. A bus driver heard me scream and he yelled at Charles who ran away.

What is the most logical order of these statements?

A) 6, 1, 3, 5, 4, 2

B) 2, 4, 5, 3, 1, 6

C) 1, 3, 4, 2, 6, 5

D) 4, 3, 5, 2, 6, 1

3. Officer Alexander has just finished interviewing the victim of an armed bank robbery.

The victim made the following statements:

1. While working as a Teller at Steward Savings and Loan, I noticed Frank Jones on line. He looked nervous.

2. Frank Jones ran out of the bank with a brown bag full of money.

3. Frank Jones produced a note demanding money and displayed a shiny pistol.

4. I showed up to work at 8:30 that morning.

5. After Frank Jones left, we closed the bank and called the police.

6. I saw Frank Jones hanging around the bank before we opened that morning.

What is the most logical order of these statements?

A) 6, 1, 3, 5, 4, 2
B) 2, 4, 5, 3, 1, 6
C) 1, 3, 4, 5, 2, 6
D) 4, 6, 1, 3, 2, 5

4. You are a police officer assigned to the 73rd Precinct. Your commanding officer has just distributed a laminated card with instructions for cardiopulmonary resuscitation. The instructions on the card include the following five statements:

I. After contacting emergency medical personnel, position the victim. To open the person's airway, turn him or her on his or her back, supporting the head and neck.

II. Before performing mouth-to-mouth breathing, look, listen and feel for respiratory movement.

III. To ascertain if someone requires CPR, gently shake the shoulder of the person who collapsed and shout, "Are you okay?" If there is no response, begin chest compressions.

IV. When performing chest compressions, press hard, fast, and deep at a rate of at least 100 beats per minute.

V. If the person does not respond, call 911 before performing CPR.

If you place the above statements in the most logical order, which step should be performed immediately AFTER shaking, tapping or talking to the victim to ascertain if he or she requires CPR?

A) Begin chest compressions
B) You should call 911.
C) You should position the victim on their back.
D) You should feel for a pulse.

The process for signing in to work is as follows:

I. All officers must report to the precinct 30 minutes prior to the beginning of their tour.

II. All officers must sign in at the front desk with the desk sergeant.

III. Officers may then get dressed in their official uniform.

IV. Officers must report to roll call no later than 15 minutes prior to the beginning of their tour for inspection.

V. After inspection, all officers assemble in the Ready Room where the sergeant will brief the officers for the tour.

VI. At the exact minute the tour begins, the officers will be dismissed to begin their tour.

VII. Any lateness must be reported immediately to the desk sergeant.

5. After reporting to the precinct, the officer must first

A. assemble for inspection
B. sign in with the desk sergeant
C. get dressed in official uniform
D. go to the ready room

6. An officer reports to roll call 13 minutes before the start of their tour. What must they do first?
A. get dressed
B. report for inspection
C. report lateness to desk sergeant
D. continue and report lateness after roll call

7. After briefing, what occurs?
A. The officers put on official uniform
B. The officers sign in
C. The officers are inspected
D. The officers are dismissed

If an individual has no heartbeat or pulse, a police officer should first remove the victim from the mechanism of injury and then initiate CPR (cardiopulmonary resuscitation). Once a victim's heartbeat and breathing are restored, other injuries can be treated. Degrees of seriousness in descending order are bleeding wounds, shock and broken bones. Minor cuts and abrasions would, of course, have the lowest priority.

8. Of the conditions listed below, which would be the one that should be treated last?
a) deep bleeding wound
b) no heartbeat
c) sprained ankle
d) shock
e) minor cuts

9. Determine the order in which you would treat the injuries described above.

a) e, b, c, a, c
b) b, a, d, c, e
c) c, b, d, a, e,
d) a, b, e, d, c
e) d, a, b, e, c

The order of procedure for signing out a patrol car is as follows:

I. Request a vehicle from the fleet supervisor

II. Examine the exterior of the vehicle for visible damage. If any is noted, inform the fleet supervisor immediately.

III. Check the oil, washer fluid, transmission fluid, and brake fluid. Note any deficiencies to the mechanic in charge.

IV. Check the tires for visible damage and check the pressure. If the pressure is below 35 psi, the officer must add air to the tires.

V. Once checked, the officer must sign the vehicle out of the lot.

10. After checking the tires for damage, what should the officer do next?

A check oil
B. sign out vehicle from lot
C. check washer fluid
D. check tire pressure

11. After requesting a vehicle from the fleet supervisor, what should the officer do next?

A. examine the exterior
B. check brakes
C. check tire pressure
D. sign vehicle out

12. If an officer checks the tire pressure, and it reads 36 psi, what should he/she do next?

A. let some of the air out
B. check the oil
C. check for damage to the tires
D. sign the vehicle out of the lot

13. If an officer checks the oil and finds it to be low, what should that officer do next?

A. notify the fleet supervisor
B. add oil
C. notify mechanic in charge
D. take another vehicle

14. If an officer is checking the exterior of a vehicle and notes a large dent on the driver's side, the officer should...

A. locate the last officer to use the car and make them report it
B. take the car and report it after the shift
C. find another vehicle
D. notify the fleet supervisor

15. Of the following four names, which is the 3rd name in alphabetical order?
A. Jones
B. Janes
C. James
D. Johns

16. How many series of the letters in **Column A** are identical to the corresponding series of letters in **Column B**?

Column A	**Column B**
aehatahasrh	aehathahasrh
gjhirbjhrg	rgjhirbjhrg
eruohbegeaeuo	eruohbegeoaeuo
ghghfdhssh	ghghfhdhssh

A. 0
B. 1
C. 2
D. 4

17. If every fourth letter of the alphabet was crossed out, what would be the new 4th letter?
A. E
B. F
C. G
D. H

18. If every second letter of the alphabet was crossed out, what would be the new 7th letter?
A. G
B. H
C. M
D. Q

19. If the digits of the smallest of the following numbers were reversed, what would the second digit be?

3876876   387886   3878667   3887897

3876376   2878861   3878967   3887899

A. 2

B. 4

C. 7

D. 8

20. Which digit in the following list of digits appears *first* for the *fifth* time?
092384572904578092857290578293045780239457823049587

A. 0

B. 2

C. 4

D. 8

21. If the alphabet were reversed, what would be the 4th letter after the letter P?

A. F

B. G

C. K

D. L

22. If the alphabet were reversed, what would be the 3rd letter after the letter Q?

A. N

B. M

C. O

D. D

23. Which letter is as far beyond the letter F as Z is beyond X?

A. I

B. L

C. J

D. H

24. Which of the even digits in the following list occurs most often?

8725497154934651973561923746152394765497643578

A. 2

B. 4

C. 6

D. 8

Answers:

1.A, 2. C, 3. D, 4. A, 5. B, 6. C, 7. D, 8. E, 9. B, 10. D, 11. A

12. D, 13. C, 14. D, 15. D, 16. A, 17. A, 18. C, 19. C, 20. B

21. D, 22. A, 23. D, 24. B

Part II, Work Styles Personality Test

The *Work Styles Questionnaire* contains a series of 74 short statements. The purpose of this part of the exam is to assess certain personality traits that have been shown to support the efforts of law enforcement. Take a minute to think about what character traits might make a good police officer. Some traits might include: assertiveness, ethical behavior, bravery, but not reckless, reliability, and a leader who can also follow directions. Also, keep in mind, that the job of police officer requires good "people skills". Officers must have the ability to keep their composure, remain calm, and project emotional stability in difficult situations. The desire to help people is also paramount.

The questions in this section go very quickly. It is very important that you keep a positive attitude about yourself during the questions, but do not try to paint yourself in an overly positive light. There is a deception scale built into this test, so you will lose points for trying to cheat. Answer honestly and completely. There are no "wrong" or "right" answers.

This assessment is closely modeled from the "Big 5" psychological exam, and it and assesses the following dimensions of personality: conscientiousness, agreeableness, emotional stability (neuroticism), interpersonal competence (emotional intelligence), and truthfulness. The exam has its roots in the MMPI and CPI exams, which are more comprehensive in their ability to detect workplace personality concerns. Items are very short and are answered quickly. The key is to be honest and consistent during the exam. Do not over-analyze the questions, and avoid devoting excessive time to any one question. Furthermore, realize that the exam is very limited in its ability to provide an accurate picture of your personality.

How Personality Measured

Psychologists define personality as, "The particular pattern of behavior and thinking that prevails across time and contexts, and differentiates one person from another." In trying to understand behavior patterns, psychologists attempt to identify and measure individual personality characteristics, often called personality traits. In 1990, psychologists Costa & McCrae published details of a 5 trait model or "Big 5". This theory is now widely accepted among psychologists and is the basis for this section of your exam.

Each of these 5 personality traits describes a person's feelings, thoughts, or behaviors. Everyone possesses all 5 of these traits along a spectrum. For example, two individuals could be described as conscientious, but there could be significant differences in the degree to which a person is conscientious.

The 5 personality traits tested are:

Extraversion – the degree to which a person is outgoing.
Persons scoring high on this trait like to work with others, are talkative, enthusiastic, and seek excitement. They work well as members of a team. People who score low on this trait work better alone, and the can be perceived by others as cold and difficult to understand.

Agreeableness – the degree to which a person has amiable relationships with others.
Those who score high on this trait are cooperative, follow direction well, and are concerned with others' feelings. People who score low are viewed as assertive, aggressive, and intolerant.

Conscientiousness – the degree to which a person is organized and reliable.
People who score high on this trait are productive, disciplined, and dependable. They thrive in structured environments. People who score low on this trait are less organized, but they can be more flexible, adaptable, and good at multitasking.

Neuroticism – the degree to which a person experiences fearfulness when confronted with new experiences and stress.

People who score high on this trait are prone to panic, experience anxiety, and can be frozen by fear. People who score low on this trait are calm, steady and rational. They are perceived as solid but sometimes unemotional or mechanical.

Openness to Experience- the degree to which a person is receptive to new ideas and experiences.

People who score high on this trait are eager to learn and are intellectually curious. People who score low on this trait are practical, slow to change, and take comfort in tradition.

All 5 personality traits exist on a continuum. Most people exhibit a range of each trait.

When thinking about personality traits, it is important to ignore the positive/negative associations that these words have in everyday language. For example, conscientiousness is seen as a positive attribute, yet a person who scores very high on this trait may not be adaptable. A police officer must be reliable and disciplined, yet able to rapidly adapt tactics to evolving situations.

Tips for Answering Questions about Honesty and Integrity

Police Officers are entrusted with testifying in court and frequently stand witness against individuals charged with crimes. It is imperative that police officers can be trusted to report information accurately and truthfully. Questions concerning honesty are apparent and should be answered without any indication of past dishonest behavior.

You should strongly agree with all of the following types of questions:

Most people are honest by nature.

You never stole as a child.

Most people can be trusted.

Most people never steal at work.

Even young people who shoplift should be punished.

Most people have never shoplifted.

Workers who leave work early without permission are stealing.

If someone is undercharged in a store, he/she should return the money.

You should strongly disagree with all of the following types of questions:

It is OK to cut out of work early, if your job is done.

It is human nature to steal from others.

Laws against stealing are too severe.

Most people cannot be trusted.

It is normal for young people to shoplift.

You need to present yourself as having a transparent moral compass. Never admit to doing drugs (or associating with people who do drugs) or having committed even minor crimes.

Tips for Answering Questions about Anger

Anger in the workplace has become an important issue in law enforcement. Lately, pre-employment investigations are closely focusing on past workplace conflicts and domestic abuse situations. Departments across the country have begun looking seriously at anger related issues in the workplace. Now, the many departments assess candidates for preexisting anger issues.

Questions concerning anger should also be answered without any ambiguity. You should affirm that you do not have latent anger issues. And further, you consider demonstrations of anger in the workplace unacceptable. Respond strongly against questions involving revenge, retribution, and mean spirited practical jokes. If you have a documented personal history of anger related issues, you need to be able to clearly demonstrate the means by which you overcame those issues. If asked in any way, answer with disapproval to all forms of workplace hostility.

You should strongly agree with all of the following types of questions:
I never become angry at work.
People who know me would say I am very patient.
I cannot remember the last time I lost my temper.
People who get angry at work should receive counseling or be dismissed.

You should strongly disagree with the following types of questions:
My colleagues agitate me.
It's normal to lose your temper at work or at home.
I get angry at stupid drivers.

Tips for Answering Questions about Stress

Police Officers are often placed in very stressful situations. They frequently encounter people at their worst, and they are exposed to physical stressors including: heat, cold, and exertion.
Validate your coping skills and indicate that you are free of stress-induced health concerns.

You should strongly agree with all of the following types of questions:

I do not worry about how well I'm doing at my job.

I never take criticism from my supervisor personally.

I have a great relationship with my colleagues.

I have confidence in my ability to do my job well.

I have never suffered physical illness due to stress.

I never get headaches from my job.

You strongly disagree with all of the following types of questions.

Work is a huge stressor.

I don't feel I am doing a good job.

My supervisor's criticisms are hurtful.

I have been counseled for stress.

I lose sleep thinking about problems at work.

You need to show that you can respond to stressful situations calmly, perform well, and move on with your work without experiencing unhealthy levels of stress.

While answering questions, keep in mind that probationary police officers are expected to do the following things:

become a member of an existing team

request assistance from another team member or supervisor

offer information and assistance to a coworker

do one's share of the work including menial tasks

show respect for authority figures (including those with more experience)

work without direct supervision

arrive on time and maintain a schedule

take responsibility for one's own actions

maintain high ethical standards

obey orders promptly

follow all rules and procedures

seek training or assistance when learning new tasks
follow safety rules and avoid unnecessary risks
master work skills and continue learning new skills
accept criticism without taking it personally
ask questions, even if it will show a lack of knowledge
maintain professional appearance at all times
maintain composure in frightening and disturbing situations
interact with different cultures, sexes, races, religions in a respectful manner convey a trustworthy and professional image in the face of physical difficulty

The questions in this section go very quickly. It is critically important that you keep a positive attitude during the examination. Do not try to overtly portray yourself in an excessively positive light. There is a deception scale built into this test, so you will lose points for trying to cheat. Answer consistently. There are no "wrong" or "right" answers.

You will read a short statement. Then, decide the degree to which you agree or disagree with each statement by selecting a rating from 1 to 5.
Choose "unsure" ONLY when you are truly not sure how to rate yourself.
Avoid spending too much time over-analyzing any single statement.
Respond to every statement, even if you are unsure or the question seems bizarre. Leaving even a few questions blank may disqualify you from the selection process.
Remember, these questions are looking for moderate responses unless the question is an obvious "red flag". Bear in mind, the exam is looking to select emotionally balanced candidates.

Strongly Disagree	Disagree	Unsure	Strongly Agree	Agree
①	②	③	④	⑤

The following practice questions give you an idea of what to expect from questions that assess your personality traits. They are very similar to what you will see on the actual exam. Rate each response with a 1-5. Once completed, look back over the questions, and ask yourself what the overall impression this gives of your personality. Don't be concerned with the numerical score; it will not translate into any meaningful conclusion. Finally, when thinking back to the questions, ask yourself how honest you feel about your responses.

Set a timer for 20 minutes, and do your best to respond to the following statements rating each 1-5.

I am very goal oriented.

I work best independently.

I am concerned about other peoples' motives for doing things.

I like to be in control of situations.

Before I act, I carefully analyze every aspect of the situation.

I can express my true feelings only when I drink.

I very seldom have spells of the blues.

I am often said to be hotheaded.

I often worry.

I do not like to tell people about myself.

My friends describe me as very helpful.

I frequently ask people for advice.

I don't make long term-plans.

I often must sleep over a matter before I decide what to do.

People have often misunderstood my intentions, when I was trying to put them right and be helpful.

I am usually calm and not easily upset.

I would feel satisfaction in solving crimes.

My boss would say I am very reliable.

It bothers me to have someone watch me at work even though I know I can do it well.

I am often so annoyed when someone tries to get ahead of me in a line that I speak to that person about it.

I "lose it" with rude people.

I am afraid of different kinds of people.

I would love to drag race.

I follow laws, even if I don't agree with them.

I love to gamble.

I thrive on taking risks.

I enjoy amusement park rides.

I like to speak in public.

I like to be the center of attention.

I am a physical person.

I respect my superiors.

I change jobs often.

I only take medication when it is prescribed to me.

I am irritable and angry.

I frequently got suspended from school for fighting.

I would lie to protect a friend.

If my friend got in trouble, I would do whatever it took to get him/her out of it.

I am a direct communicator.

I am easily convinced of a good idea.

I would rather figure something out for myself than read the instructions.

My grades in school were excellent.

I try to be diplomatic with difficult coworkers.

I am a low-key person.

I enjoy working with my colleagues.

I need to be commended by my supervisor for a job well done.

I have a quick temper.

I generally do good work.

I pretend to be compassionate to the concerns of others.

I am very secure in my opinions and beliefs.

I never failed a class in school.

I am optimistic about the future.

I like high end jewelry and cars.

I am very open to new ideas and points of view.

I am afraid of wild animals.

I have a strong pain threshold.

I almost never give up on a problem.

I hate to be hurried.

I am not afraid of roaches.

I feel a sense of dread and unease much of the time.

Many days, I have trouble getting out of bed.

I take great satisfaction in fixing things around the house.

I can "read" how other people are feeling.

I am afraid of travelling through tunnels.

I am afraid of wide open spaces.

I sometimes feel that I am going to lose control.

I am never frightened of the dark.

I like to plan ahead.

Often I get nervous in front of people and forget what I want to say.

I really like playing team sports (such as soccer or softball).

I hate my whole family.

People say it's hard to get to know me.

I am approachable.

When someone does something that makes me angry, I let them know how I feel about it.

I can take insults without lashing out.

The next set of questions focuses on your past work experiences. Answer honestly and consistently with your verifiable past. Keep in mind you may face an interview with a psychologist later in the application process. The psychologist may ask about your responses to verify them against your application. After the exam, make notes about the questions and how you responded. Being consistent with your responses will make the process much smoother for you.

1. How many times in the past year have you called in sick to work to take care of personal business?

A. never
B. once
C. twice
D. three times
E. more than three times

2. Your previous supervisor would describe you as someone who usually does:

A. more than your fair share of the work
B. more work than most of your coworker
C. about as much work as most of your coworkers
D. almost as much work as most of your coworkers
E. less work than most of your coworkers

3. In the past year, what dollar amount of office supplies have you taken from your job for personal use?

A. none
B. $1.00- $50.00
C. $51.00- $99.00
D. $100.00- $150.00
E. more than $150.00

4. Within the past two years, how many times have you taken a day off because you did not feel like going to work?

A. never
B. once
C. twice
D. three times
E. more than three times

5. How much time during your workday do you spend making personal phone calls?

A. none
B. less than 15 minutes
C. 15-30 minutes
D. 30-60 minutes
E. more than 1 hour

6. How much work time do you spend using social media during the work day?

A. none
B. less than 15 minutes
C. 15-30 minutes
D. 30-60 minutes
E. more than 1 hour

7. How much work time do you spend on fantasy sports websites sites during the work day?

A. none
B. less than 15 minutes
C. 15-30 minutes
D. 30-60 minutes
E. more than 1 hour

8. How many days in the past two years have you called in sick because you were hung over?

A. none
B. 1-2
C. 3-4
D. 5-6
E. more than 6

9. How many jobs have you had in the past 5 years?

A. 1
B. 2
C. 3-4
D. 4-6
E. More than 6

10. Have you ever been fired with cause from a job?

A. Yes
B. No

11. How many days a month do you volunteer outside of work?

A. 0.
B. 1 - 2
C. 3 - 5
D. 6 - 8
E. 9 or more

12. How skilled are you at your job?

A. overly skilled
B. quite skilled
C. moderately skilled
D. slightly skilled
E. not at all skilled

13. How professionally do you behave?

A. extremely professionally
B. quite professionally
C. moderately professionally
D. slightly professionally
E. not at all professionally

14. How honest are you with your coworkers?

A. brutally honest
B. very honest
C. moderately honest
D. slightly honest
E. not at all honest

15. How well do you share responsibility for tasks with your coworkers?

A. perfectly
B. very well
C. fairly well
D. slightly well
E. not at all well

16. How well does your supervisor work with members of the public?

A. perfectly
B. very well
C. moderately well
D. fairly well
E. not at all well

17. How do you view work-related meetings?

A. essential
B. important
C. somewhat important
D. time better spent working
E. a complete waste of time

18. How fairly are responsibilities shared among your coworkers?

A. perfectly
B. quite fairly
C. moderately fairly
D. mostly unfair
E. totally unfair

19. How do you view your supervisor?

A. a great leader
B. an effective leader
C. no opinion
D. dead weight
E. a hindrance

20. How often do your meet your deadlines?

A. always
B. most of the time
C. half of the time
D. rarely
E. never

21. How polite are you with your coworkers?

A. overly polite
B. quite polite
C. moderately polite
D. slightly polite
E. rude

22. How comfortable are you challenging your supervisor?

A. extremely comfortable
B. comfortable
C. moderately
D. slightly
E. not at all

23. How quickly do you adjust to changing priorities?

A. instantly
B. quickly
C. moderately quickly
D. slowly
E. never

24. How quickly do you act on decisions?

A. instantly
B. quickly
C. moderately quickly
D. slowly
E. never

25. How would describe your work habits?

A. workaholic
B. very hardworking
C. somewhat hardworking
D. slightly hardworking
E. lazy

26. Overall, how effective are you at your job?

A. extremely effective
B. quite effective
C. moderately effective
D. slightly ineffective
E. completely ineffective

27. How well do you work with other coworkers?

A. extremely well
B. very well
C. moderately well
D. slightly well
E. not at all well

28. How quickly do you follow up on requests from supervisors?

A. immediately
B. quickly
C. somewhat quickly
D. slowly
E. almost never

29. How detail oriented are you in your work?

A. I am a perfectionist.
B. I give my work a lot of attention to detail.
C. I give my work a moderate amount of attention to detail.
D. I give my work little attention to detail.
E. I do not give my work any attention to detail.

30. How well do you handle criticism at your job?

A. I thrive on it.
B. I can see its value.
C. I can tolerate some of it.
D. I refuse to accept it.

31. How quickly do you adjust to changing priorities?

A. instantly
B. very quickly
C. moderately quickly
D. reluctantly
E. not at all

32. How hard do you work to meet the goals you set for yourself?

A. extremely hard
B. quite hard
C. somewhat hard
D. not very hard
E. not at all

33. How much confidence do you have in your ability to make the right decisions?

A. total confidence
B. a lot of confidence
C. some confidence
D. little confidence
E. no confidence at all

34. How satisfying is your current work?

A. totally satisfying
B. very satisfying
C. moderately satisfying
D. a little satisfying
E. not satisfying at all

35. How challenging is your current job?

A. extremely challenging
B. very challenging
C. somewhat challenging
D. rarely challenging
E. not at all challenging

36. In a typical week, how often do you feel stressed at work?

A. constantly
B. very often
C. somewhat often
D. rarely
E. never

37. How many times in the past 6 months have you returned from a break late?

A. never
B. 1-2 times
C. 3-4 times
D. 5-6 times
E. more than 6 times

38. How well do your coworkers value your input and ideas?

A. a great deal
B. a lot
C. somewhat
D. rarely
E. never

39. How realistic are the expectations of your supervisor?

A. perfectly realistic
B. very realistic
C. somewhat realistic
D. rarely realistic
E. not at all realistic

40. How often do the tasks assigned to you by your supervisor help you grow professionally?

A. constantly
B. most of the time
C. somewhat often
D. rarely often
E. never

41. How motivated are you to earn a promotion?

A. totally motivated
B. very motivated
C. somewhat motivated
D. a little motivated
E. not motivated at all

42. The ideal work environment for you is…

A. completely independent
B. a mixture of independent and team tasks
C. somewhat supervised
D. always paired with another coworker
E. constantly supervised

43. How often do you require praise for a job well done?

A. constantly
B. very often
C. somewhat often
D. rarely
E. never

44. How often have you left work early in the past 6 months?

A. never
B. 1-2 times
C. 3-4 times
D. 5-6 times
E. more than 6 times

45. How proud are you of the type of work you do?

A. very proud
B. moderately proud
C. neutral, don't care
D. not very proud
E. not at all proud

46. How much do you respect your current employer?

A. respect very much
B. respect a moderate amount
C. neutral, don't care
D. do not respect very much
E. do not respect at all

47. How often are you late for work in a 3-month period?

A. never
B. 1-2 times
C. 3-4 times
D. 4-5 times
E. 6 or more times

Glossary

Accessory: One who is not the chief actor in the offense, nor present at its performance, but is in some way involved, either before or after the act committed. One who aids, abets, commands, or counsels another in the commission of a crime. Synonym for "accomplice" or "abettor."

Admission: Generally, confessions, concessions or voluntary acknowledgments made by a person of the existence of certain facts. In the criminal context, a statement by a person of facts which in connection with proof of other facts or circumstances, tends to prove guilt, but which is, of itself, insufficient to merit conviction.

Aggravation (offense; e.g. aggravated assault, aggravated battery): Any circumstance attending the commission of a crime which increases its guilt or enormity or adds to its injurious consequences, but which is above and beyond the essential constituents of the crime itself.

Arrest: To take a person into custody, by authority of law, for the purpose of charging him/her with a criminal offense.

Arrest Warrant: A written order issued by a judge that directs a law enforcement officer to arrest a person and bring them to court.

Arson: Burning or attempting to a burn a building owned by another, with the intent to kill or seriously injury a person.

Assault: An attempt or threat to inflict bodily injury upon another, along with the apparent ability to do so, which places the victim in fear of injury or bodily harm.

Attempted Robbery: A crime that results in no property taken but the suspect is still sought for the actions leading to the attempt.

Back Up: Police officers who assist the first responders.

Battery: Battery is causing bodily harm to a person by any means, or making physical contact with a person of an insulting or provocative nature.

Bench Warrant: A document issued by the court to mandate the appearance of an individual before the court.

Blood Alcohol Concentration (BAC): The concentration of alcohol in the bloodstream.

Breathalyzer: An instrument used by trained operators to measure the Blood Alcohol Content (BAC) of a person's breath.

Burglary: Entering a dwelling, room, or building of another with the intent to carry away items or fixtures from the premises.

Carjacking: Knowingly or recklessly by force or violence, taking or attempting to take from another person immediate actual possession of the person's motor vehicle.

Child: A person who has not yet attained the age of 16 years old.

Citation: An order issued by the police requiring a person to appear on a specific day and do something therein mentioned.

Civil Action: A lawsuit to redress a private wrong, in which the remedies are money damages and/or injunctions.

Coercion: The threat or use of mental or physical means to get information.

Community Stakeholders: All individuals and organizations that have a vested interest in a safe and healthy community. This includes public and private institutions, social service providers, schools, churches, businesses, property owners, renters, and others.

Complainant: The victim, the arresting officer, or the person or agency filing a complaint.

Complaint: A statement, under oath, whereby a witness accuses an individual of criminal behavior.

Confession: A person's admissions of enough facts to establish his or her guilt of a particular crime.

Conspiracy: Agreement with another, or others, to commit a crime, and an act by any party to the agreement in furtherance of the agreement.

Contempt: An act that constitutes a violation of a court order or disrespect toward the judge or the court proceedings.

Controlled Substance: A drug or substance regulated by federal or State law, including opiates and hashish.

Court: A tribunal having authority under the Constitution to settle disputes.

Court Appointed Attorney: An attorney appointed to represent an indigent defendant or other indigent litigant.

Crime Triangle: A tool used in problem-solving. The sides of the triangle – victims, offenders, and the location – represent the three elements of every crime situation. The crime triangle is used in problem solving to foster a thorough analysis of crime patterns and more effective actions that will reduce the harm caused by a problem.

Criminal Action: A lawsuit in which the state or the public, rather than a private party, is plaintiff, and the defendant faces punishment such as a fine or incarceration if convicted.

D.O.A.: Abbreviation for "dead on arrival" as applied to a person who expires before reaching a medical facility.

D.O.B.: Abbreviation for "date of birth."

Delinquent: A person under the age of 18 who has been adjudicated for an act that would be a crime if committed by an adult, and who requires guidance, treatment, and rehabilitation.

Detective: A sworn member of the Department responsible for the follow-up investigation of crime.

Disorderly Conduct: An act which unreasonably alarms or disturbs another and provokes as breach of the peace.

Distribution of a Controlled Substance: Knowingly and intentionally transferring or attempting to transfer a controlled substance to another person.

Driving Under the Influence (DWI): Driving while intoxicated with alcohol.

Duress: Forcible restraint or restriction.

Evidence: Oral statements, documents, sound and video recordings, and objects admissible in court. To be admissible, evidence must be material (it must go to a substantial issue in the case) and relevant (it must go to the truth or falsity of a matter asserted).

Extradition: The surrender by one state to another of an individual accused or convicted of an offense outside its own territory and within the territorial jurisdiction of the other, which being competent to try and punish him, demands the surrender.

Felony: An offense for which a sentence of death or a term of imprisonment for one year or more is provided.

Field Sobriety Test: Tests of coordination given at the time and on the scene of a traffic stop to assist in determining if an individual is intoxicated.

Frisk: A limited protective search for concealed weapons and/ or dangerous instruments. Usually it occurs during a "stop" and consists of a pat down of the individual's clothing to determine the presence of weapons or other dangerous objects. An officer may frisk a person on the basis of "reasonable suspicion" that the person is carrying a concealed weapon or dangerous instrument.

Homicide: The unlawful killing of a human being, including murder and manslaughter.

Homicide, Justifiable: A homicide based on the perpetrator's reasonable belief that he/she had no alternative but to use deadly or substantial force to protect himself/herself from immanent death or great bodily harm, or to prevent a forcible felony.

Indictment: An accusatory document presented by a grand jury to the court, charging a named individual with a crime.

Intimidation: To threaten another in order to influence his behavior. The threat may include physical harm, restraint, confinement, or accusations of crime (even if true).

Jurisdiction: The geographic range of authority.

Juvenile: A person under 18 years of age.

Lockup: A temporary detention facility. While in lockup, the prisoner is photographed and fingerprinted.

M.O.: Abbreviation for modus operandi, Latin for method of operation. The pattern of behavior which is typical of how a particular offender commits a specific type of crime. Example: An offender who always wears dark glasses when robbing banks.

Manslaughter: Unlawfully killing a human being without malice.

Manslaughter, Voluntary: Killing a human being with the intent to kill or do serious bodily injury, or with a conscious disregard of an extreme risk of death or serious bodily injury, where the presence of mitigating factors (e.g. acting in the heat of passion caused by adequate provocation) precludes a determination that the killing was malicious.

Manslaughter, Involuntary: An unintentional or accidental killing without justification or excuse.

Minor: In the criminal context, a person under the age of 18 years. Also see juvenile.

Misdemeanor: An offense punishable by one year of imprisonment or less.

Murder, First Degree: The killing of another with the specific intent to kill that person, with premeditation and deliberation, and without self-defense or mitigation.

Murder, Second Degree: The killing of another with the specific intent to kill or seriously injure that person, or acted in conscious disregard of an extreme risk of death or serious bodily injury to that person, and without self-defense or mitigation.

Negligent Homicide: The killing of another as a result of the careless, reckless, or negligent operation of a motor vehicle.

Offense: A violation of the criminal law of a state or local jurisdiction.

Petty Offense: An offense for which the only allowable penalty is a fine.

Polygraph: A lie detector.

Possession of a Controlled Substance: Knowingly and intentionally possessing a controlled substance.

Probable Cause: Where known facts and circumstances, of a reasonably trustworthy nature, are sufficient to justify a man of reasonable caution or prudence in the belief that a certain person has committed, is committing, or is about to commit a criminal act.

Problem: A problem suitable for police/community resolution has the following characteristics: it is a group of related incidents; it affects a number of people; it is unlikely to disappear without intervention; a number of people agree to work on it; and it can be impacted with available resources.

Prosecutor: An attorney who brings a criminal action against a person in the name of the government.

Radar: Portable unit used by officers to determine speeds of approaching vehicles in the field.

Rape: The crime of sexual intercourse with a subject by force or threat of force, against the will and without the consent of the subject.

Reasonable Suspicion: A combination of specific facts and circumstances that would justify a reasonable officer to believe that a certain person had committed, is committing, or is about to commit a criminal; more than a hunch or mere speculation but less than probable cause necessary to arrest.

Recidivist: A repeat offender.

Roll Call: The first part of a watch or tour, reserved for attendance, inspection, briefings, and training.

Search Warrant: A written order signed by a judge authorizing an officer to search for and seize property that constitutes evidence of commission of a crime.

Sexual Abuse: Engaging in a sexual act or sexual contact with another person with knowledge or reason to know that the act was committed without that other person's permission

Shoplifting: (1) Knowingly concealing or taking possession of personal property of another that offered for sale; or (2) removing or altering the price tag, serial number or other identification mark imprinted on or attached to personal property of another, which was offered for sale; or (3) transferring any personal property of another, which was offered for sale, from the container in which it was displayed or packaged to any other display container or sales package.

Statute of Limitations: The period of time within which lawsuits or criminal prosecutions must be brought, after which it is barred for lapse of time. There is no limitation on when a prosecution can be brought for murder.

Theft: Wrongfully obtaining or using the property of another person with the intent of depriving the person of a right to the property or appropriate the property to his or her own use or to the use of another person.

Traffic Ticket: Ticket issued by a police office for a traffic infraction that one can either pay or appear in court to plead or argue.

Trajectory: The path a bullet or other flying object takes.

Unlawful Entry: Intentionally entering or attempting to enter a building without lawful authority and against the will of the occupant or the person in charge of the premises.

Verbatim: Word for word.

VIN: Abbreviation for "vehicle identification number," a unique identifier assigned when the vehicle is manufactured.

Warrant: A written order issued by a judge that directs a law enforcement officer to arrest a person and bring them to court.

Witness: One who testifies as to what they have seen, heard, or otherwise observed and who is not necessarily a party to the action.

Youth: A person under the age of 18, also referred to as a juvenile.

Demographic Information

- New Jersey has 8,900,000 people.
- The State capital is Trenton.
- The State's largest city is Newark with 275,000 people.
- Per Capita income in 2008 was $54,699, which made it second highest in the United States.
- New Jersey is a major intersection along the Northeast corridor. As such, its roads serve as major arteries for trade and transportation. The New Jersey Turnpike and Garden State Parkway are cultural icons as much as they are roads.
- New Jersey has major harbors along the Delaware and Hudson rivers.
- There are 10 densely populated counties within the state.
- Most law enforcement agencies in New Jersey follow a military format: Police Officer, Sargent, Lieutenant, Captain, Major, Colonel.
- Promotions for Sargent, Lieutenant, and Captain are generally through promotional exams. Other positions are appointed by the Police Commissioner.
- Law enforcement in New Jersey is very diverse. From serving in high-crime urban areas such as Newark and Camden to small town, rural areas in the west and south, New Jersey offers a wide range of experiences.